CW00505046

Mercedes-Benz

CARS OF THE 1990s

Other titles in the Crowood AutoClassic Series

Mercedes–Benz

CARS OF THE 1990s

JAMES TAYLOR

THE CROWOOD PRESS

First published in 2009 by
The Crowood Press Ltd
Ramsbury, Marlborough
Wiltshire SN8 2HR

www.crowood.com

© James Taylor 2009

All rights reserved. No part of this publication may be reproduced
or transmitted in any form or by any means, electronic or mechanical,
including photocopy, recording, or any information storage and retrieval
system, without permission in writing from the publishers.

**British Library Cataloguing-in-
Publication Data**
A catalogue record for this book is available from the British Library.

ISBN 978 1 84797 096 1

Designed and edited by Focus Publishing,
11a St Botolph's Road,
Sevenoaks,
Kent TN13 3AJ

Printed and bound in Malaysia by Times Offset (M) Sdn Bhd

Contents

Introduction
and Acknowledgements

Once upon a time, a Mercedes was a medium-sized saloon, a luxury saloon or an expensive roadster. However, all that changed during the 1990s. Although it was a fascinating period for observers of the marque, it was also in many ways a disheartening one, for, alongside the new ranges that were introduced to broaden the marque's appeal, there came a very noticeable deterioration in quality. A Mercedes had once been for ever; now, it seemed, it would deteriorate just as quickly as any other car.

Fortunately, the marque pulled through, although its reputation was undoubtedly tarnished in the process. Quality did improve again as the twenty-first century got under way, and it became possible once again to look back on the 1990s as a Mercedes enthusiast and not to flinch at the memory.

This book is all about the cars that Mercedes built during the 1990s. It does not dwell on the reliability and build quality issues of the time, but rather looks at what was available, at the characteristics of the models, and at the way in which each range fitted into the overall Mercedes jigsaw. It is written from the point of view of an enthusiast, but it does not ignore the wider business issues which affected the direction that the marque took in the last decade of the twentieth century.

Many people have helped me put this work together. Among them are several owners, and I must thank especially those members of the Mercedes-Benz Club in the UK who provided photographs of their cars, namely Pete Lewis at Cheshire Classic Benz (www.ccbenz.co.uk), Nik Grewer and Tim Imrie. Over in the USA, my colleague Kevin Girling provided a good number of press shots and some useful information.

I do not pretend that this book is definitive, because each one of the ranges it covers could merit a book on its own. However, I hope it will provide enthusiasts with a good background overview of a momentous period in Mercedes history, and will encourage readers to look more closely into some of the cars from that period. Despite their undeniable faults, they are for the most part classic Mercedes that are every bit as deserving of the three-pointed star as their predecessors.

James Taylor
Oxfordshire, August 2008

1 Mercedes-Benz in the 1990s

Expanding the Ranges

There are many people who are convinced that the 124 series cars, built between 1985 and 1997, were the 'last real Mercedes'. Others, perhaps those with a wider knowledge of the marque, would vote for the 129 roadsters (1989–2000) or the 140-series saloons and coupés (1992–1998). The fact that these views and others like them are so widespread is clear witness to a single truth: something radical happened to the Mercedes-Benz marque during the 1990s.

The usual complaints from long-time devotees of the marque are that quality declined and that engineering excellence took a back seat to style and fashion. Both criticisms are, regrettably, largely justified, but it is important to understand the context in which Daimler-Benz decided to make the changes in its Mercedes-Benz car division, which led in turn to these changes in its products.

In fact, more than one radical thing happened in the 1990s, and the roots of those radical changes can be traced back to the 1980s. Before 1982, Mercedes-Benz had depended primarily on three car ranges (plus, from 1979, the G-Wagen off-roader). Those three car ranges were its medium saloons, its S class luxury saloons, and its SL sports models. Within these ranges were related derivatives, such as the estate and coupé derivatives of the medium saloons or the big coupés based on the S class cars. In 1982 the new 190 range added a cheaper and smaller entry-level model to the Mercedes line-up – and it proved to be a huge success.

Even within Daimler-Benz, there were those who had their doubts about whether the 190s were 'proper' Mercedes, so it is not hard to imagine how they reacted to the idea that there should be an even wider range of Mercedes models in the 1990s. Yet the 1990s came to be characterized by more new-model launches than any previous decade in Mercedes history. Between 1995 and the arrival of the M class SUV in 1998, for example, the company launched ten new cars – a statistic that compares strikingly with the three new models launched in the decade that immediately preceded that.

The 1990s saw the line-up of ranges expanded by no fewer than four – the A class, the CLK, the SLK and the M class – on top of the existing five (C, E, S, SL and G). By adding in the newly renamed CL class (originally subsumed within the S class), it could be argued that the number of Mercedes model ranges doubled during the 1990s – and it would continue to expand in the decade that followed.

Under Pressure

A key factor behind these changes was the fact that the 1980s saw the Mercedes marque under more pressure from its rivals than ever before. Particularly striking was the dramatic rise of BMW, which had been an also-ran in the 1960s, but in less than twenty years had fought its way to a position that threatened Mercedes' long-established dominance of the German domestic market. Not far behind was the Audi division of Volkswagen – and these two were only the domestic competitors.

Central to the Mercedes line-up as the 1990s opened was the W124 range, and central to that range in turn was the saloon model. It provided variants ranging from taxi to luxury barge. Seen here is a 1994 model with the injected 2-litre M102 engine. By this time, the range had been renamed E class – so this is an E200 – and had been facelifted with a flush-mounted grille.

Significantly, both had much wider model ranges than Mercedes. The only way for the Stuttgart manufacturer to keep ahead was therefore to fight on a broader front than before and to introduce new model ranges alongside its existing ones.

These rivals threatened not only Mercedes sales, but also the Mercedes image. Both BMW and Audi had managed to make their cars appeal to a younger and more style-conscious audience and, while there were many stylish Mercedes models, there was a strong feeling that Mercedes were making cars for older and more staid customers. The BMW business model in particular demonstrated the value of brand loyalty: the company had a clever strategy in place which captured a customer in his or her 20s and then provided an appealing

model to match every upward step in that customer's career. Without a model to capture the younger customer – even the 190 range was distinctly staid and expensive enough to be beyond the reach of the average 25-year-old – Mercedes was bound to lose out in the longer term.

When Edzard Reuter took over from Werner Breitschwerdt as Chairman of Daimler-Benz AG, on 1 September 1987, it was clear that he would have to steer the Mercedes car brand towards a wider coverage of the market. It was also clear that the traditional Mercedes would have to be joined by cheaper models with deliberate appeal to younger customers. Breitschwerdt could see that the very structure of the company as it was then might hinder this change, and so he was instrumental in giving the Mercedes car division more management autonomy during 1989. From 29 June that year, Daimler-Benz AG became the umbrella organization of which Mercedes-Benz AG was a separately managed part, along with AEG AG (the domestic appliance division) and Deutsche Aerospace AG (the aerospace division).

In charge of Mercedes-Benz AG was Werner Niefer, and on taking office he was almost immediately confronted with a new challenge. Nobody knew how serious the threat from Toyota's new Lexus brand, announced that year, would be – but there was absolutely no doubt that the Japanese company was gunning for Mercedes' dominance of the world luxury-car market with its new luxury saloon. The new Lexus was clearly intended to compete head-on with the

existing W126 S Class models. Mercedes did have its new W140 under development for introduction in 1991, but there was no cause for complacency.

In fact, not long after the new S Class was announced, Mercedes revealed its extreme vulnerability to another problem. This time, it was an economic recession that affected the Western world. Suddenly, large and expensive luxury cars were no longer in demand, and nowhere was this trend more noticeable than in the market which had for several decades been Mercedes' most important – North America. Sales of the new S Class slowed right down, and sales of other Mercedes models were affected by fluctuations in international exchange rates. The result was a severe shock to the Mercedes finances.

As a result, the writing was on the wall at

The W202 C class was the first range to incorporate the new customer-centred Mercedes philosophy. This is a 1995 UK-spec car.

Stuttgart by the end of 1992. When Helmut Werner took over from Werner Niefer at the helm of Mercedes-Benz AG, on 27 May 1993, his priorities were clear. He had to continue the model diversification initiated by his predecessor in order to protect the company against sudden downturns in the luxury-car market. In order to remain competitive with rivals from both Germany and Japan, he had to cut manufacturing costs. And in order to keep Mercedes competitive in the USA, and to reduce the likely effects of currency fluctuations in that huge and very important market, he had to give the marque a manufacturing base in North America. The company also had to meet new challenges in other markets, such as those of the former Soviet Bloc, which were now opening up to foreign imports; not least of them was the former East Germany.

Over the next few years, Werner pushed through the necessary changes, with the assistance of Jürgen Hubbert, head of the passenger car division, and Dr Dieter Zetsche, head of product development (who would himself head Mercedes-Benz AG a decade or so later).

A Re-Think

The changes that the Mercedes management had identified as necessary demanded a significantly different way of thinking at Stuttgart. The Mercedes-Benz car division had traditionally been run by its engineers, but it was clear that what was best in engineering terms might not always offer the maximum customer appeal. Young buyers, in particular, were more likely to be swayed by such things as stylish interiors than by sensible engineering solutions. In future, customer demand would be paramount because expansion of sales was essential for the company's long-term survival.

Expansion of sales would also be driven by new model ranges, and, in order to finance these, costs would have to be saved in the development and production areas. Development lead-times would also have to be

The W202 models had the new Mercedes family look right from the beginning, with the three-pointed star mounted on the bonnet panel rather than on the grille.

Mercedes in the USA

Could a Mercedes-Benz built outside Germany be a real Mercedes-Benz? Despite suspicions to the contrary, the evidence was compelling: CKD manufacture of Mercedes models using parts shipped out from Germany had been going on successfully for years. Although there were concerns among conservative elements within the company, an assembly plant was established in Alabama, USA, during 1994 to go one step further and manufacture complete cars from scratch.

The key reason was that the biggest market for Mercedes' new ML class SUV (*see* Chapter 10) was going to be the USA, and it made best sense to manufacture the vehicle in-territory rather than to add to its cost by shipping examples from Germany.

In fact, some manufacture of the ML class was still carried out in Germany. The new Alabama plant was run by a newly formed subsidiary called MBUSI (Mercedes-Benz USA, Inc), which bought engines and transmissions from the parent company in Germany and sold complete vehicles back to them, all in dollars. The system not only simplified accounting but also helped to protect Daimler-Benz against currency fluctuations.

reduced in order to get these new ranges on to the market in time to meet the company's business targets; one of these targets was to become the number-one German manufacturer by the year 2000.

It was unfortunate, though probably inevitable, that such radical changes would have a negative impact on the products. It soon become clear from the new models introduced in the mid-1990s where Mercedes had done its cost-cutting, and traditional customers soon began to complain about falling standards. Not everybody was convinced that the new American factory, opened to build the new M class sports utility model in the heart of what was expected to be its biggest market, could deliver Mercedes quality. And the build quality problems that afflicted the Mercedes cars of the later 1990s continued well into the next decade, doing incalculable harm to the hard-won Mercedes image in the process.

Yet, by the end of the 1990s, Mercedes management had achieved most of the aims it had set itself seven years earlier. The marque had re-invented itself and was widely perceived as offering many models of interest to the younger buyer, and at the same time it had not deserted its traditional clientele. Careful brand imaging had persuaded most potential customers to believe that the Mercedes name still stood for the best quality available in the automotive world, even though there was no shortage of unlucky (and vociferous) souls who were disappointed enough to raise their voices in protest at what had happened.

The Chrysler Alliance

Meanwhile, the Daimler-Benz company as a whole continued to evolve. On 24 May 1995, Jürgen Schrempp took over from Edzard Reuter as the Daimler-Benz Chairman, and he oversaw a further restructuring on 1 April 1997, when the Mercedes car division was once again taken into Daimler-Benz AG. In May 1998 came another radical move: a merger with the American Chrysler Corporation.

Mercedes quality certainly declined in the late 1990s and did not pick up again until the middle of the following decade. This rust on a six-year-old W210 is mild compared with some cases, and Mercedes replaced without charge panels on a number of cars that had been badly affected.

Chrysler had been ailing in the North American marketplace for some time, and it quickly became apparent that what had been billed as a merger was really more of a Daimler-Benz takeover. Nevertheless, the proprieties were respected with the adoption of the new name of 'DaimlerChrysler' for the newly merged companies, and their products remained very distinct and very separate. Unless, that was, customers looked too closely at the mechanical specification of vehicles such as the Jeep Grand Cherokee, which began to sport Mercedes diesel engines in place of the bought-in ones it had used in earlier times...

In fact, the DaimlerChrysler merger was nowhere near as successful as its chief architect Jürgen Schrempp had hoped. For Daimler-Benz, it had looked like an opportunity to enter the volume end of the car market in a single step, and so spread the costs of new technology – particularly the electronics systems in which Daimler-Benz was a world leader – over a much bigger output. Unfortunately, it took a very long time to turn Chrysler around, and the brand did not record a profit until 2005. In the meantime, the stock-market value of the two brands began to fall, and the wedded DaimlerChrysler ended up worth less than Daimler-Benz had been worth before the merger. By 2007 it was all over: Mercedes and Chrysler parted, although the German company retained a percentage holding in its former American ally.

Engineering

As a result of the turn to more fashionable car designs in the 1990s, development times had to become shorter in order to get new products on to the market quickly, while the long model-cycles of traditional Mercedes-Benz practice became a thing of the past. Yet a great deal of the same engineering thinking remained in place.

In particular, the Mercedes marque aimed to get ahead of the competition in the emerg-

Mercedes in Motorsport

Motorsport has almost always figured somewhere in the Mercedes-Benz world view, and the 1990s saw the marque score a number of notable successes. Throughout the decade, beginning in October 1990, the company's motorsport activities were overseen by Norbert Haug.

In the touring car championships featuring cars derived from those covered in this book, Mercedes put up some strong performances. Klaus Ludwig was German Touring Car Championship (DTM) winner in 1992 with a 190E 2.5-16 Evo 2, and again in 1994, driving an AMG-Mercedes C class. In 1995 Bernd Schneider won both the DTM and International Touring Cars championships with an AMG-Mercedes C class, and in 1997 and 1998 AMG-Mercedes won both the drivers' and team championships in the FIA GT class.

Mercedes returned to Formula 1 racing in 1994, providing engines for the McLaren team cars. In 1998, Team McLaren-Mercedes won the Constructors' World Championship. That same year, and for a second time in 1999, driver Mika Hakkinen won the Formula 1 Drivers' World Championship at the wheel of a McLaren-Mercedes.

An alliance with McLaren led to Formula 1 success – and later to an astonishing new road car, too.

13

ing field of electronic systems. It took a few years for the new designs to be ready for production, but from 1997 cars began to appear with a whole array of new electronic systems. These affected everything from safety to traction and gear-changing aids, providing a degree of automatic control of a number of on-board systems that had simply not been attainable earlier. New acronyms such as BAS (Brake Assist System) and ASSYST (a service interval indicator) entered the Mercedes vocabulary.

After the turn of the century, electronics allowed the marque to introduce new equipment that gave it a technological edge over its rivals. Unfortunately, the late 1990s saw a prolonged period of teething troubles, and a lack of reliability in some early electronic systems did nothing for the Mercedes reputation. It was all very well being a world leader in the new technology, but if that new technology failed to work, customers found it an irritation rather than a benefit.

As had always been the case, common componentry was used wherever possible across the various model ranges to simplify servicing and spares logistics, and to save both development and engineering costs. Gearbox design was a case in point and, while five speeds with an overdrive top remained the norm for manual gearboxes, automatics changed from four speeds in the first half of the 1990s to five speeds, also with an overdriven top, as the decade progressed.

Particularly interesting was the evolution of Mercedes engine design over this decade. As the 1990s began, the Mercedes strategy was to share components between the four-cylinder and six-cylinder petrol engines, while the V8s had their own componentry. However, the strategy for the next generation of engines was to move from in-line six-cylinder engines to V6 types, and to share componentry between the V6s and the V8s. There was a further complication, too, which was the expansion of the range to include a V12.

The move to V6 engines resulted from a piece of characteristically Mercedes clear thinking. Some model ranges would use four-, six- and eight-cylinder engines, and so their engine bays needed to be designed around the longest of these. The V8s were only marginally longer than the four-cylinders, and it was the six-cylinders that demanded the extra length. However, by changing to a vee format for the sixes, the engine length would be reduced so that it would fit into the same space as the fours and V8s. This would enable Mercedes to save weight by reducing engine bay length, provide the opportunity for better crash management at the front of the car, and allow better packaging of the passenger and luggage compartments within a given overall vehicle length.

After the turn of the century, similar thinking would be used for the new diesel engine ranges, but for the 1990s the plans were different. There would be three 'families' of related engines, all in-line types with four-cylinder variants for the small diesels, five-cylinder types for the mid-range models, and six-cylinder types (both with and without turbochargers) for the largest sizes. The development in Mercedes diesel thinking would be seen in areas other than the architecture of the cylinder blocks.

The Diesels

Mercedes entered the 1990s with the OM601, OM602 and OM603 engines in production. All had indirect injection and the same 84mm bore and 87mm stroke. The OM601 was a 2-litre four-cylinder, the OM602 a 2.5-litre five-cylinder, available with and without a turbocharger, and the OM603 was a 3-litre six-cylinder, also available with or without a turbocharger. From 1993, a 3.5-litre turbocharged OM603 was also made available, and was the only one of the family to have different bore and stroke dimensions.

This first family was gradually phased out from 1993, although the last ones did not go out of production until 1999. Their replace-

*A UK-registered C140 S500 coupé
dating from the 1995 model-year
(pictures kindly supplied by Pete Lewis
at Cheshire Classic Benz).*

ments were the OM604, OM605 and OM606, which brought four-valve technology to the diesel engine but retained indirect injection. Once again, the five-cylinder (OM605) and six-cylinder (OM606) types were available both with and without turbochargers. Swept volumes were the same as they had been in the earlier engines.

The big step forward, however, came in 1997 with the first engines to use common-rail direct injection. This delivered the fuel to the cylinders at very high pressure, and electronic metering ensured that precisely the right amount was injected into the individual cylinder at precisely the right time. This made for more efficient combustion, which gave both better economy and big increases in power and torque. The CDI (Common-rail Direct Injection) family of engines that featured this were the OM611, OM612 and OM613 types; all were turbocharged.

Perhaps most important for Mercedes' manufacturing was the fact that the electronic control system of the new CDI engines was tuneable in a way that diesel engines had not been tuneable before. So, for example, the 2.2-litre OM611 four-cylinder could be used in 102PS form for the 200 CDI models and in 125PS form for the 220CDI types. Altering the software in the engine control unit to deliver less

power was far cheaper than building a smaller-capacity engine with a whole collection of different components.

CDI technology was also used for the new OM668 four-cylinder that was designed specially for the A class models, which expanded the Mercedes range downwards towards the end of the 1990s. To save manufacturing costs, a single 1.7-litre capacity was used, but different states of tune enabled the delivery of outputs of between 60PS and 95PS. And as the new century opened, Mercedes was ready with its new OM628 4-litre twin-turbocharged V8 diesel, which again used CDI technology and heralded a move into another new area.

Four-Cylinder Petrol Engines

The four-cylinder petrol engines in production at the start of the 1990s were the M102 family, which covered a capacity range from 1.8 to 2.3 litres. From 1992, however, these engines were gradually replaced by the new M111 four-cylinders, which had the latest four-valve architecture, to improve breathing and efficiency. The range once again covered capacities from 1.8 to 2.3 litres, but one important factor deriving from Stuttgart's overall engine strategy was that all these engines

ABOVE, RIGHT AND OPPOSITE: The R170 (SLK) range successfully brought the Mercedes roadster to a new audience.

had the same 89.9mm bore, and that they shared this with the new M104 six-cylinders. This link between the new 'fours' and the revised versions of the existing 'sixes' allowed for a number of valuable manufacturing economies.

However, the four-cylinder engines took a big step forward in the middle of the decade. To get more sporting acceleration from these relatively small-capacity engines, and so provide a credible alternative to BMW's small six-cylinders, Stuttgart's engineers turned to forced induction. They ruled out turbocharging because the off-boost performance of a turbocharged engine was invariably disappointing, and instead chose to use supercharging.

The supercharger (known to Mercedes as the Kompressor) was belt-driven from the engine, and could therefore always be called upon to deliver its boost. Its installation was not like that on the supercharged Mercedes of the 1930s, however, where the supercharger had to be engaged by means of its own clutch. The new Kompressor was permanently engaged, with just an electro-magnetic clutch to disengage it automatically and prevent engine damage in certain conditions. It arrived on the 2-litre M111 engine in 1995 and on the 2.3-litre type a year later.

A very different line of small-capacity petrol engines was initiated for the A class range in 1997. These were the M166 types, designed as lightweight engines and for transverse installation. They remained unique to the A class in this period, although they were later seen in related van and MPV models.

The In-Line Petrol Sixes

As the 1990s began, Mercedes had three different six-cylinder petrol engines in production. Two of these were M103 types with a single overhead camshaft: the 166bhp 2.6-litre and the bigger-bore 3-litre with 190bhp. The third was the company's first multi-valve six-cylinder. Introduced in 1989, the M104 24-valve engine was a development of the M103 featuring twin overhead camshafts with variable valve timing and four valves per cylinder. At the start of the decade, this ancestor of a new range of engines came with the same 3-litre capacity as the larger M103 (and the same bore and stroke dimensions), but it put out 231bhp.

The M103s did not last long. From September 1992, they gave way to new M104 DOHC engines, this time a 197bhp 2.8-litre and a 220bhp 3.2-litre. At the same time, the 24-valve 3-litre engine, which had proved somewhat harsh at high revs, was dropped from production.

Early V8 Petrol Engines

Meanwhile, there were also three families of V8 engine in production: the M116, M117 and M119 types. The M116s and M117s were the oldest of these, the M116 coming with capacities of 3.8 and 4.2 litres, while the M117 came as a 5-litre or 5.6-litre.

The M119s were created by adding four-valve cylinder heads and variable camshaft timing to these older engines, beginning with the 5-litre in 1989 and going on to the 4.2-litre in 1992. In each case, the bore and stroke dimensions remained unchanged.

Mercedes and AMG

As the demand for bespoke, high-performance derivatives of Mercedes models rose in the 1990s, so the market for the specialist tuners such as Carlsson and Brabus expanded. These companies produced some stupendously powerful high-performance engines with appropriate other modifications to match, but their products were built in small numbers and at a very high cost.

Ever since the late 1960s, Mercedes had worked closely with AMG, and the expanding market for high-performance models in the 1990s made very clear the advantages of this arrangement. So from 1999, Mercedes took a controlling interest in AMG, which effectively became its in-house high-performance division. Its job was to counter the M-badged Motorsport cars from BMW, the S-badged performance models from Audi, and the R-badged cars from Jaguar.

AMG worked closely with Mercedes on competition cars during the 1990s, but its road engines are probably more widely known. The Mercedes M104 straight-six was developed into a punchy 280PS 3.6-litre from 1994, while the M119 V8 could be had as a 376PS 6-litre from 1993, a 306PS 4.3-litre from 1998, and a 347PS 5.5-litre from 1999. Supercharging arrived for the 3.2-litre M112 V6 in 2000, and the AMG-developed engine delivered the same 347PS as the 5.5-litre V8, which would later be supercharged itself to deliver 500PS. Even the M120 V12 was developed to produce a 525PS 7.3-litre engine from 1999.

The V6s and Later V8s

The new M112 V6 and M113 V8 engines arrived in 1997 and were built on the same assembly lines at an all-new factory in Bad Cannstadt. They shared a 90-degree vee configuration, two spark plugs per cylinder and three valves per cylinder. It was a configuration that was found by Stuttgart's engineers to deliver better results than the earlier four-valve configuration. The V6s alone had a counter-rotating balancer shaft that turned at crankshaft speed to damp out vibrations from the less-than-ideal configuration: most V6s have a 60-degree included angle between the cylinder banks because this gives the smoothest running characteristics.

They were also considerably lighter than the engines they replaced; for example, an M112 V6 was 25 per cent lighter than the M104 in-line six of the same capacity. The cylinder blocks were of lightweight construction, being pressure die-cast from aluminium and magnesium, and they had silicon cylinder linings instead of conventional metal liners. These silicon linings also lowered noise and improved the heat flow around the crankcase. Also noteworthy were the 'cracked' steel connecting rods, whose big ends were cracked and re-joined for precision during manufacture because this gave better results than machining.

There were 2.8-litre and 3.2-litre M112 V6s, which were direct replacements for the M104 in-line sixes of the same capacity. But the M112 range also included a 2.4-litre derivative that gave Mercedes a six-cylinder engine to compete more effectively with BMW's small sixes in that sector of the market.

...And the V12s

Right at the top of the engine range, the 1990s brought a new departure. As long as the only V12 engine in an S class competitor had been made by Jaguar, Stuttgart had not been too concerned, but when BMW introduced a V12 engine in 1987, it was clear that there would have to be a Mercedes equivalent. From 1991 there was: the M120 was a 6-litre engine with two overhead camshafts on each cylinder bank, four valves per cylinder and a massive 394bhp.

It was only to be expected that this engine would also pioneer new technologies, and in fact it presaged the later M112 V6s and M113 V8s in the use of all-alloy construction with silicon cylinder liners to save weight. The engine was in effect built as two six-cylinders sharing a common crankshaft, and each bank of cylinders had its own electronic control system.

The engine bay of the SLK32 AMG.

The M120 V12 had a relatively short life. It was massively complicated, and for its successor Stuttgart decided to simplify the design. The 60-degree angle between the cylinder banks stayed the same, but the new M137 had to be shorter to fit in to the engine bay of the W220 S class, which had been designed around the V8 engines. As a result, it had a longer stroke, to compensate for the reduced bores necessitated by a shorter cylinder block. It was some 80kg (175lb) lighter, and had a slightly smaller capacity of 5.8 litres along with lower power and torque outputs. This was feasible because the cars it was to power were lighter.

Like the M112 V6s and M113 V8s, it had three valves and two spark plugs for each cylinder, together with roller tappets and just one overhead camshaft on each cylinder bank. Its electronic control system also enabled the left-hand cylinder bank to be shut off at light loads below 3000rpm to save fuel.

Image

Absolutely fundamental to Mercedes thinking in the 1990s was the need to turn the company's image around. Despite its hard-won and long-established reputation as a maker of reliable, durable and safe cars, Stuttgart was suffering in the marketplace because rival makers were offering more exciting machinery. It had been clear since the 1980s and the introduction of the W201 190 range that Mercedes needed to appeal more to a younger clientele, and with the 1990s that need to appeal to younger buyers intensified.

Inevitably, this forced the company to focus more on performance, handling and style than it ever had done before. It was this thinking which led to a change in the relationship between Stuttgart and leading Mercedes tuner AMG (*see* sidebar on page 18) and which led at the end of the decade to AMG becoming in effect the high-performance arm of the Mercedes organization. It was this thinking that led to the creation of the SLK roadsters (*see* Chapter 8), lay behind the ill-fated involvement in the Smart venture (*see* sidebar on page 20), and was probably a factor in switching the mid-size coupés from the medium saloon (or E class) platform to that of the compact saloons (or C class).

*Top of the 'everyday'
W208 CLK range was
the V8-powered CLK430,
seen here in right-hand-
drive cabriolet form.*

It was also this thinking that led Mercedes to initiate a series of futuristic concept cars. The F100, with its central driving position, was the first of these, appearing at the 1991 Detroit Motor Show and previewing such technology as a cruise control with distance warning radar and proximity control. The F100 also pioneered the 'sandwich' floor construction that entered production six years later for the A class, and was followed by the V12-engined gullwing-doored F200 Imagination, displayed at the 1996 Paris Motor Show. The fact that its joystick controls were probably not very practical was not really the issue: what the car did was to demonstrate that Mercedes was experimenting with exciting new technology. And some of the technology that this car and others previewed would eventually appear in the Mercedes of the next decade...

The Smart Car

During the 1990s, Daimler-Benz was also associated with the Smart car, a project initiated by the Swiss watch manufacturer Swatch. The original plan was for the car to use innovative features such as a hybrid engine. It was also planned as a city car that would be short enough to allow nose-in parking and would be cheap enough to appeal to young buyers.

After abortive talks elsewhere, Swatch CEO Nicholas Hayek concluded a joint venture deal with Daimler-Benz to manufacture the car, which became known as the Smart. Micro Compact Car AG, as the joint venture was known, built a purpose-designed factory at Hambach in France in 1994 and the first Smart cars (two-seater 'city coupés' called Fortwo

models) were previewed at the 1997 Frankfurt Motor Show.

Despite strong sales, the joint venture suffered from heavy losses. Mercedes was by this stage also deeply involved with its own A class city car and the two partners fell out. In due course, Swatch pulled out altogether; then, in 2006, Smart GmbH (as it had become) was liquidated and its operations were wholly absorbed by Mercedes-Benz, which redesigned the Fortwo model before re-launching it in Europe during 2007.

The Smart car range was sold through Mercedes-Benz dealers but was always kept separate from the Mercedes brand itself.

2 Carry-Overs from the 1980s

The W124, W126 and W201 Ranges

As the 1990s opened, Mercedes was just on the brink of replacing its S class saloons and coupés, was well on the way to replacing its compact '190' saloons, and had begun to think about replacing its mid-range W124 saloons, estates and coupés. An all-new SL sports car range had been introduced in 1989 (*see* Chapter 3 for a description), and production of the ageing but evergreen G-Wagen 4×4 was showing no sign of ending.

The 'carry-over' ranges of the 1990s – the W201 '190s', the W124 mid-range cars, and the W126 S class – nevertheless still had plenty of life in them, and the last of these 1980s designs was not built until 1996. They were therefore important in helping to define what the Mercedes marque stood for during the 1990s.

The 124 Range

The strongest-selling Mercedes car range at the beginning of the 1990s was the mid-range W124. Introduced in 1985, it would end

Firm favourites from the W124 range were the two-door coupé models, arguably some of the best-looking Mercedes ever made. They were available with either four-cylinder or six-cylinder engines.

production in stages between 1994 and 1996, and would become the biggest-selling Mercedes range ever, with a total of 2.7 million cars. There were three body variants, all of them styled by Bruno Sacco: the four-door saloon, the enormously roomy and practical estate (S124), and the elegantly stylish two-door coupé (C124).

By 1 January 1990, the saloon range could be had with nine different engines: two four-cylinder petrol models (200E and 230E), three six-cylinder petrol models (260E, 300E and 300E-24), one small-volume V8 petrol model (500E), one four-cylinder diesel (200D), one five-cylinder diesel (250D), and two six-cylinder diesels (300D and 300D Turbo). With the exception of the naturally aspirated 3-litre diesel and the 5-litre V8, all those engines were also available in the estates, which carried an additional T in their model names; thus, the estate version of the 300E, for example, became a 300TE.

The two-door cars, however, were available only with petrol engines. Most markets had one four-cylinder engine (230CE) and two six-cylinders (300CE and 300CE-24), but some countries had the option of a four-cylinder 200CE to suit local taxes on engine size.

An Extra Body Style

All this began to change in 1991, and that autumn a fourth body style was introduced: a two-door cabriolet (A124), developed from the C124 coupé. All the first cars were left-hand-drive 300CE-24 six-cylinders, but right-hand-drive cars and a four-cylinder model did become available a year later. Like the other 24-valve models, the cabriolets all had the latest design of eight-hole alloy wheels; the coupés, meanwhile, continued with steel wheels and plastic trims as standard or with 16-hole alloys as an option – although in the UK and some other countries the alloys were standard wear.

The cabriolet's body shell was very recognizably derived from the coupé type, but it incorporated more than 1000 new or redesigned panels, which ensured that neither crash safety nor torsional rigidity was compromised by the loss of the fixed roof. This strengthening made the car heavier than other 124-range models, but the extra weight did not have a very noticeable effect on performance.

It was perhaps typical of the Mercedes approach that the cabriolets did not come with

The W124 range was almost infinitely adaptable! This is the factory's own six-door model, usually used for private hire or by hotels. Some examples were also created by aftermarket coachbuilders, who stretched a standard four-door model.

a power-operated roof, although this was an extra-cost option. Even then, the catches on the screen header rail had to be operated by hand. Equally typical of Mercedes was the superb fit and finish of the convertible top. It came with a heated rear window made of tinted glass at a time when many convertible models still had a Perspex window. When erected, the hood was every bit as sleek as the fixed roof of the C124 coupé, but when stowed it took up an embarrassingly large proportion of the boot space. Customers could order an extra-cost removable wind deflector to fit behind the front seats, but this did make the rear seats unusable.

However, the key feature of the cabriolets used technology pioneered on the R129 SL range in 1989. Where the SL had a self-erecting rollover bar behind the seats, which sprang into position to protect the occupants when sensors and the central microprocessor detected that the car was about to turn over, the A124 cabriolet had a pair of rear head restraints that performed the same function. Perhaps it was no surprise, then, that the cabriolets always came with a formidably high price tag.

1992: The Four-Valve Petrol Engines

This was only the beginning: the next two years were to see even more far-reaching changes to the 124 range. First came a new saloon-only derivative in early 1992, badged as a 400E. To a large extent, this was intended to cater for those who had found themselves too far down the waiting list for the limited-production 500E, but it also made a W124 super-saloon available in the USA, where the 500E had not been homologated for sale. The 400E had the 272bhp 4.2-litre four-valve V8 engine from the SL sports cars and the W140 S class saloons, which were new at the time. In European form, it could hit 60mph in 7 seconds, while US models had a taller final drive, to improve fuel economy and avoid the 'gas-guzzler' tax, and were therefore slightly

> ### The AMG W124 Models
>
> Alongside the standard showroom versions of the W124 range, Mercedes' favoured tuner AMG offered saloons, coupés and even estates with their own 3.6-litre high-performance derivative of the M103 3-litre engine.

slower. The 400E was rather less complicated than the 500E. Although it had the same engine bay modifications, it did not have the wider transmission tunnel or the flared wheel arches, and it was built on the lines at Sindelfingen rather than sub-contracted to Porsche at Zuffenhausen.

Next, at the Frankfurt Show in autumn 1992, came a new range of petrol engines. These were all four-valve types with twin overhead camshafts, and completely replaced the existing four-cylinder and six-cylinder engines. The four-cylinders belonged to the new M111 family, and came as a 136bhp 2-litre and a 150bhp 2.2-litre, which created the new 200E and 220E models respectively. The sixes came as a 197bhp 2.8-litre in the new 280E, which replaced both the old 260E and the 300E, and as a 220bhp 3.2-litre, which replaced the old 300E-24. The latter engine had first been seen in the W140 S class models in 1990.

Mercedes claimed that the four-valve layouts had been developed mainly to give more efficient combustion, with better control of exhaust emissions and improved fuel economy as two of the more desirable results. Torque increases in the lower rev ranges also played their part in delivering better acceleration and fuel economy. There was new technology, too: all the new engines had electronic management systems, with high-tension distributors that had no moving parts, and a single twin-spark ignition coil for each cylinder. Careful design had also saved weight and had kept noise levels some two decibels below those of the older two-valve engines.

The cabriolet version of the W124 range was developed from the two-door coupé, and had a heavily reinforced body shell to compensate for the absence of a fixed roof. This was a full four-seater car (although the rear passengers did not enjoy a lot of room), and quickly took on the prestige always associated with open Mercedes of that configuration.

All the new four- and six-cylinder engines had the variable inlet camshaft timing pioneered on the 300CE-24's six-cylinder engine, and came with catalytic converters as standard. The new sixes had the new 'resonance variable inlet manifold', where a pneumatically controlled flap divided the inlet system into two three-cylinder sections below about 4000rpm. This improved gas flow at low and medium engine speeds, and contributed to better torque right across the rev range. Both the six-cylinder engines could be had with the five-speed automatic transmission pioneered on the 24-valve 300E models.

There were cosmetic changes in the autumn 1992 update, too: the old sixteen-hole alloy wheels were replaced on all models by the latest eight-spoke design already seen on the top W124 derivatives. Meanwhile, other upgrades filtered through from the W140 S class cars. These included the automatic dipping rear-view mirror, infra-red remote central locking, an improved anti-theft system, and modified air conditioning, which allowed heated air to flow through the dashboard's central vents. A driver's-side airbag became standard, together with electric adjustment for the driver's door mirror, while thicker door

glass improved sound insulation. All these changes affected the diesel models as well as the petrol derivatives, but it would be another year before their engines were updated.

1993: A Name Change, a Facelift, and Four-Valve Diesels

Mercedes used the Frankfurt Show in October 1993 to showcase another major round of changes. What had once been simply the mid-range Mercedes now became the E class for the 1994 and subsequent model-years. Boot-lid badges changed to reflect this, and the petrol-engined models were now badged as E200, E220, E280, E320, E420 and E500. The coupés, cabriolets and estates lost their distinctive badge lettering in this process, becoming simply E220 or E320 models.

At the same time, the appearance of the cars was freshened by the addition of a frameless grille recessed into the bonnet panel. This followed the lead set by the W140 S class and picked up by the new W202 C class, introduced in June 1993. Bumper and front apron were restyled slightly to suit, and clear front indicator lenses replaced the amber items. Steel-wheeled cars now had new six-hole plastic trims, and interior trim was brightened

Specifications for 1990s W124 Models

Engines

Petrol saloons

200	1997cc M102 4-cyl, 105PS & 158Nm	(1989–1990)
200E	1997cc M102 4-cyl, 118PS & 172Nm	(1989–1992)
	1998cc M111 4-cyl, 136PS & 190Nm	(1992–1993)
E200	1998cc M111 4-cyl, 136PS & 190Nm	(1993–1995)
220E	2199cc M111 4-cyl, 150PS & 210Nm	(1992–1993)
E220	2199cc M111 4-cyl, 150PS & 210Nm	(1993–1996)
230E	2299cc M102 4-cyl, 132PS & 198Nm	(1989–1992)
260E	2599cc M103 6-cyl, 160PS & 220Nm	(1989–1992)
280E	2799cc M104 6-cyl, 197PS & 270Nm	(1992–1993)
E280	2799cc M104 6-cyl, 193PS & 270Nm	(1993–1995)
300E	2962cc M103 6-cyl, 180PS & 255Nm	(1989–1992)
300E-24	2960cc M104 6-cyl, 220PS & 265Nm	(1989–1992)
320E	3199cc M104 6-cyl, 220PS & 310Nm	(1992–1993)
E320	3199cc M104 6-cyl, 220PS & 310Nm	(1993–1995)
400E	4196cc M119 V8, 279PS & 400Nm	(1991–1993)
E420	4196cc M119 V8, 279PS & 400Nm	(1993–1995)

Petrol saloons

500E	4973cc M119 V8, 326PS & 480Nm	(1991–1992)
	4973cc M119 V8, 320PS & 470Nm	(1992–1993)
E500	4973cc M119 V8, 320PS & 470Nm	(1993–1995)
AMG E60	5956cc M119 V8, 381PS & 470Nm	(1993–1994)

Diesel saloons

200D	1997cc OM601 4-cyl, 75PS & 126Nm	(1989–1993)
E200 Diesel	1997cc OM601 4-cyl, 75PS & 126Nm	(1993–1995)
250D	2497cc OM602 5-cyl, 94PS & 158Nm	(1989–1993)
	Oxidation cat model with 90PS	(1990–1993)
E250 Diesel	2497cc OM605 5-cyl, 113PS & 173Nm	(1992–1996)
250D Turbodiesel	2497cc OM602 5-cyl, 126PS & 231Nm	(1988–1993)
E250 Turbodiesel	2497cc OM602 5-cyl, 126PS & 231Nm	(1993–1995)
300D	2996cc OM603 6-cyl, 113PS & 191Nm	(1989–1993)
	Oxidation cat model with 110PS	(1990–1993)
E300 Diesel	2996cc OM606 6-cyl, 136PS & 210Nm	(1993–1995)
300D Turbodiesel	2996cc OM603 6-cyl, 147PS & 273Nm	(1988–1993)
E300 Turbodiesel	2996cc OM603 6-cyl, 147PS & 273Nm	(1993–1995)

Petrol estates

200T	1997cc M102 4-cyl, 105PS & 158Nm	(1989–1990)
E200	1998cc M111 4-cyl, 136PS & 190Nm	(1993–1996)
200TE	M102 4-cyl, 118 PS & 172Nm	(1989–1992)
	1998cc M111 4-cyl, 136PS & 190Nm	(1992–1993)
220TE	2199cc M111 4-cyl, 150PS & 210Nm	(1992–1993)
E220	2199cc M111 4-cyl, 150PS & 210Nm	(1993–1996)
230TE	2299cc M102 4-cyl, 132PS & 198Nm	(1989–1992)

continued overleaf

Specifications for 1990s W124 Models *continued*		
Engines *continued*		
280TE	2799cc M104 6-cyl, 197PS & 270Nm	(1992–1993)
E280	2799cc M104 6-cyl, 193PS & 270Nm	(1993–1996)
300TE	2962cc M103 6-cyl, 180PS & 255Nm	(1989–1992)
300TE–24	2960cc M104 6-cyl, 220PS & 265Nm	(1989–1992)
320TE	3199cc M104 6-cyl, 220PS & 310Nm	(1992–1993)
E320	3199cc M104 6-cyl, 220PS & 310Nm	(1993–1996)
E36 AMG	3606cc M104 6-cyl, 272PS & 385Nm	(1993–1996)
Diesel estates		
200TD	1997cc OM601 4-cyl, 75PS & 126Nm	(1989–1991)
250TD	2497cc OM602 5-cyl, 94PS & 158Nm	(1989–1993)
	Oxidation cat model with 90PS	(1990–1993)
E250 Diesel	2497cc OM605 5-cyl, 113PS & 173Nm	(1993–1996)
250TD Turbodiesel	2497cc OM602 5-cyl, 126PS & 231Nm	(1990–1993)
E250 Turbodiesel	2497cc OM602 5-cyl, 126PS & 231Nm	(1993–1996)
300TD	2996cc OM603 6-cyl, 113PS & 191Nm	(1989–1993)
	Oxidation cat model with 110 PS	(1990–1993)
E300 Diesel	2996cc OM606 6-cyl, 136PS & 210Nm	(1993–1996)
300TD Turbodiesel	2996cc OM603 6-cyl, 147PS & 273Nm	(1988–1993)
E300 Turbodiesel	2996cc OM603 6-cyl, 147PS & 273Nm	(1993–1996)
Coupés		
200CE	1997cc M102 4-cyl, 122PS & 178Nm	(1990–1992)
	Catalyst model with 118PS & 172Nm	
	1998cc M111 4-cyl, 136PS & 190Nm	(1992–1993)
E200 Coupé	1998cc M111 4-cyl, 136PS & 190Nm	(1993–1996)
220CE	2199cc M111 4-cyl, 150PS & 210Nm	(1992–1993)
E220 Coupé	2199cc M111 4-cyl, 150PS & 210Nm	(1993–1996)
230CE	2299cc M102 4-cyl, 132PS & 198Nm	(1989–1992)
300CE	2962cc M103 6-cyl, 180PS & 255Nm	(1989–1992)
300CE–24	2960cc M104 6-cyl, 220PS & 265Nm	(1989–1992)
320CE	3199cc M104 6-cyl, 220PS & 310Nm	(1992–1993)
E320 Coupé	3199cc M104 6-cyl, 220PS & 310Nm	(1993–1996)
E36 AMG Coupé	3606cc M104 6-cyl, 272PS & 385Nm	(1993–1996)
Cabriolets		
E200 Cabriolet	1998cc M111 4-cyl, 136PS & 190Nm	(1993–1997)
E220 Cabriolet	1998cc M111 4-cyl, 150PS & 210Nm	(1993–1997)
300CE-24 Cabriolet	2960cc M104 6-cyl, 220PS & 265Nm	(1992–1993)
E320 Cabriolet	3199cc M104 6-cyl, 220PS & 310Nm	(1992–1997)
E36 AMG Cabriolet	3606cc M104 6-cyl, 272PS & 385Nm	(1993–1997)

Transmissions
Four-speed manual
Five-speed manual
Five-speed close-ratio manual (320E/E320, 320CE, 400E/E420 and 500E/E500 only)
Four-speed automatic
Five-speed automatic

Running gear
Front suspension with MacPherson struts, wishbones, coil springs, gas dampers and anti–roll bar.
Rear suspension with five links, coil springs, gas dampers and anti-roll bar; hydro-pneumatic self-levelling strut standard on some models and optional on others.
Power-assisted recirculating-ball steering.
Disc brakes all round, ventilated at the front on six-cylinder and V8 models; dual hydraulic circuit and servo assistance; ABS standard on some models and optional on others.
Tyres 185/65 × 15 (200, 200D); 195/65 × 15 (all other models except 400E/E420 and 500E/E500).

Dimensions
Overall length: 186.6in (saloons); 184in (coupés and cabriolets)

Wheelbase:	110.24in (saloons and estates); 106.8in (coupés and cabriolets)
Overall width:	68.5in
Overall height:	56.7in (saloons); 55.5in (coupés); 64.5in (estates)
Track:	58.9in (front); 58.6in (rear)

Weights (typical)
200:	1258kg (2778lb)
250D:	1318kg (2911lb)
260E:	1328kg (2933lb)
300CE-24 cabriolet:	1704kg (3762lb)
300D:	1368kg (3021lb)
400E:	1658kg (3660lb)
500E:	1694kg (3740lb)

up to meet the challenge from manufacturers such as BMW and Audi.

More important for the long-term future of the Mercedes marque, however, were the new four-valve diesel engines – the first to have such a configuration anywhere in the world. As with 1992's new petrol engines, the four-valve configuration had been used mainly to provide better control of exhaust emissions in anticipation of new regulations relating to diesel emissions. The engines had actually been previewed a few months earlier in the new W202 C class cars, but were no less welcome in the E class W124s for all that. There were just two of them: a 113bhp five-cylinder in the E250 Diesel and a 135bhp six-cylinder in the E300 Diesel. Neither offered quite the performance or refinement of the rival BMW diesel, but both turned out to be traditionally long-lived Mercedes oil-burners.

The Last Models

As far as the W124 saloons were concerned, the facelifted models lasted just two years, coming to an end in mid-1995 as the new

W210 saloons took over. The first W210 estates did not reach the market until a year later, however, and so the S124 models soldiered on a little longer. Last to go out of production were the C124 coupés and A124 cabriolets, which disappeared in 1996, leaving a long gap in which customer interest in their W208 replacements built up to very high levels.

There is no doubt that the 124 models were the last of their kind. They had been designed and engineered at a time when Mercedes had believed its engineers knew best, and as a result they lasted exceptionally well. The new philosophy that swept through the Mercedes car division in the early and mid-1990s placed a greater emphasis on meeting the customer's whims and on building down to a price. The new E class (*see* Chapter 6) was a very different kind of car.

The W201 Range

Mercedes' entry-level saloon, the 'compact' W201, had been introduced in 1983, deliberately designed as a competitor for

The core engine of the W201 range was the 2-litre M102 type, a four-cylinder that was directly related to the six-cylinder M103. Here it is in fuel-injected guise, as used in the 190E (which was later rebadged as a 190E 2.0).

the hugely successful BMW 3 Series. Face-lifted in 1988, it had also spawned successful racing derivatives and had played a very important role in Mercedes' profitability during the 1980s. The W201 was still regarded as a significant player in its field as the 1990s began, and more than 1.8 million examples had been built by the time production came to an end, in 1993.

The W201 only ever came as a four-door saloon. At the start of 1990, it was available in nine different models. The basic four-cylinder petrol models came as a carburettor 190, an injected 190E, and an injected 190E 2.3; the latter was not available in Britain. In the USA, the car badged as a 190E was in fact a 190E 2.3 with the injected 2.3-litre engine. There was a six-cylinder 190E 2.6, and there were two low-volume variants derived from the racing models. These were the 190E 2.5-16 and the extravagant 190E 2.5-16 Evolution II, of which only 502 were built, all in 1990. The three diesel models were the taxi-driver's favourite four-cylinder 190D,

Stuttgart competed in touring-car races with the W201s during the 1980s, and high-performance versions with the Cosworth-developed 16-valve engine were offered to the public for homologation purposes. Limited-edition 'Evo' models apart, the final showroom version was the 190E 2.5-16. Touring-car racer Klaus Ludwig saw the last example come off the assembly lines.

ABOVE: The 'small' Mercedes introduced in the 1980s was the W201, usually known as the 190. By the start of the 1990s, the models were characterized by plastic protective panels along the lower body sides. This is a 1991 model.

RIGHT: Even though the W201 was a 'small' Mercedes, its creators took care to give it all the character of their bigger models. So, although there was less room inside than in other cars from Stuttgart, there was no mistaking that this was a proper Mercedes.

BELOW: The W201 range was developed with a range of engines, in accordance with established Mercedes practice. One of the engines used was the 2.6-litre version of the six-cylinder M103, which made a quick and smooth version of the car called the 190E 2.6. Shown behind that car is the high-performance version with Cosworth-developed engine. It was a 190E 2.5-16 in the early 1990s, but had started life as the smaller-capacity 190E 2.3-16.

ABOVE: *More high-performance derivatives of the W201: a 190E 2.5-16 at the back, and in front of it the Evolution and (in the foreground) Evolution II models, which were developed as 'homologation specials' to enable Mercedes to go touring-car racing successfully.*

LEFT: *The sculpted shape at the rear of the W201 models provided good airflow to aid fuel consumption at speed. This is a 190E 1.8, with 1.8-litre engine.*

the five-cylinder 190D 2.5 and the 190D 2.5 Turbo.

By this stage, the 190 with its 2-litre four-cylinder petrol engine was the only Mercedes car without fuel injection. Yet it had always been a strong seller, so, rather than abandon

this sector of the market, Stuttgart decided to replace it with a new entry-level model that featured a smaller-capacity injected engine that delivered better fuel economy. That new model was introduced as the 190E 1.8 in mid-1990 (although not until March 1991 in the UK), and at the same time the existing 190E with its injected 2-litre engine was renamed a 190E 2.0.

The new 1.8-litre engine was a short-stroke derivative of the 2-litre M102 four-cylinder, and it delivered 109bhp as against the carburettor 2-litre's 105bhp, together with slightly more torque. However, it was not to have a long production life, lasting only to the end of W201 production in 1993, and was not carried over to the replacement W202 models.

Specifications for 1990s W201 Models

Engines

Petrol models

190E 1.8	1797cc M102 4-cyl, 109PS & 150Nm	(1990–1993)
190E (2.0)	1997cc M102 4-cyl, 118PS & 172Nm	(1986–1991)
	1997cc M102 4-cyl, 122PS & 175Nm	(1991–1993)
190E 2.3	2299cc M102 4-cyl, 136PS & 200Nm	(1989–1993)
190E 2.5-16	2498cc M102 4-cyl, 195PS & 235Nm	(1988–1993)
	Non-catalyst model with 204PS & 240Nm	
190E 2.5-16 Evolution II	2463cc M102 4-cyl, 235PS & 245Nm	(1990)
190E 2.6	2599cc M103 6-cyl, 160PS & 220Nm	(1986–1993)
	Non-catalyst model with 166PS & 228Nm	

Diesel models

190D	1997cc OM601 4-cyl, 75PS & 126Nm	(1989–1993)
190D 2.5	2497cc OM602 5-cyl, 94PS & 158Nm	(1989–1993)
190D 2.5 Turbo	2497cc OM602 5-cyl, 126PS & 231Nm	(1988–1993)

Transmissions

Four-speed manual	(190, 190D, 190E)
Five-speed manual	(190, 190D, 190E 1.8, 190E/190E 2.0, 190E 2.3, 190E 2.6, 190D 2.2, 190D 2.5, 190D 2.5 Turbo)
Five-speed close-ratio manual	(190E 2.5-16, 190E 2.5-16 Evolution II)
Four-speed automatic	(190, 190D, 190E/190E 2.0, 190E 2.3, 190E 2.6, 190D 2.2, 190D 2.5, 190D 2.5 Turbo)

Running gear

Front suspension with MacPherson struts, wishbones, coil springs, telescopic dampers and anti-roll bar.

Rear suspension with five links, coil springs, telescopic dampers and anti-roll bar; hydro-pneumatic self-levelling strut standard on some models and optional on others.

Recirculating-ball steering with optional power assistance (standard on some models).

Disc brakes all round, ventilated at the front on some models; dual hydraulic circuit and servo assistance; ABS standard on some models and optional on others.

Tyres: 185/65 × 15; 245/40ZR17 on 2.5-16 Evolution II.

Dimensions

Overall length:	174in; 174.4in (190E 2.5-16); 175in (US models)
Wheelbase:	104.9in
Overall width:	68.5in
Unladen height:	54.4in; 53.6in (190E 2.5-16)
Track:	56.2in (front); 55.7in (rear)

Weights (typical)

190 (manual):	1076kg (2376lb)
190E:	1098kg (2425lb)
	(US model 1210kg/2670lb)
190E 2.6:	1206kg (2662lb)

The W126 Models

As the 1990s began, the Mercedes flagships were the W126 S class saloon and its two-door coupé derivative. The saloons came as six-cylinder petrol 260SE and 300SE models, or as V8 petrol 420SE, 500SE and 560SE types,

with long-wheelbase 300SEL, 500SEL and 560SEL variants, plus a long-wheelbase diesel badged as a 350SDL. Not every variant was available in every country: there were no 260SE models for the UK, for example, and no right-hand-drive diesels at all. The coupés (strictly C126 types) came only with the

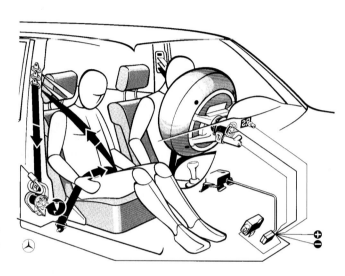

RIGHT: *Safety had long been a Mercedes preoccupation, and the W126 S class cars had been among the first to be offered with a driver's airbag.*

BELOW: *The biggest engine in the Mercedes range at the start of the 1990s was the 5.6-litre V8. It was available only in the R107 roadsters and in the W126 saloons and coupés.*

ABOVE: *The two-door coupé derivatives of the W126 were swift and luxuriously equipped models available with a variety of engines. This example is a 420SEC, with a 4.2-litre V8 under its elegant bonnet.*

Long-wheelbase versions of the S class gave Mercedes a limousine model. In tandem with the 5.6-litre V8 engine, the long-wheelbase W126 became a 560SEL. Only small numbers of standard-wheelbase cars were built with that engine.

Specifications for 1990s W126 Models

Engines

Petrol saloons

260SE	2599cc M103 6-cyl, 160PS & 220Nm	(1986–1991)
300SE	2962cc M103 6-cyl, 180PS & 255Nm	(1986–1991)
300SEL	2962cc M103 6-cyl, 180PS & 255Nm	(1986–1991)
420SE	4196cc M116 V8, 231PS & 335Nm	(1987–1991)
	Catalyst version with 224PS & 325Nm	
420SEL	4196cc M116 V8, 231PS & 335Nm	(1987–1991)
	Catalyst version with 224PS & 325Nm	
500SE	4973cc M117 V8, 265PS & 405Nm	(1986–1991)
	Catalyst version with 252PS & 390Nm	
500SEL	4973cc M117 V8, 265PS & 405Nm	(1986–1991)
	Catalyst version with 252PS & 390Nm	
560SE	5547cc M117 V8, 300PS & 455Nm	(1988–1991)
	Catalyst version with 279PS & 430Nm	
560SEL	5547cc M117 V8, 300PS & 455Nm	(1987–1991)
	Catalyst version with 279PS & 430Nm	

Diesel saloons

350SD Turbodiesel	3449cc OM603 6-cyl, 136PS & 310Nm	(1990–1991)
350SDL	3449cc OM603 6-cyl, 136PS & 319Nm	(1990–1991)

Coupés

420SEC	4196cc M116 V8, 231PS & 335Nm	(1987–1991)
	Catalyst version with 224PS & 325Nm	
500SEC	4973cc M117 V8, 265PS & 405Nm	(1986–1991)
	Catalyst version with 252PS & 390Nm	
560SEC	5547cc M117 V8, 300PS & 455Nm	(1987–1991)
	Catalyst version with 279PS & 430Nm	

Transmissions
Four-speed manual
Five-speed manual
Four-speed automatic

Running gear
Front suspension with twin wishbones, coil springs, rubber auxiliary springs, telescopic dampers and anti-roll bar.
Rear suspension with semi-trailing arms, coil springs, rubber auxiliary springs, telescopic dampers and anti-roll bar; hydro-pneumatic self-levelling strut optional.
Power-assisted recirculating-ball steering.
Disc brakes all round, with dual hydraulic circuit and servo assistance; ABS optional.
Tyres 205/65 × 15.

Dimensions

Overall length:	196.7in (SE); 202.3in (SEL and SDL); 202.6in (US-model SE); 208.1in (US-model SEL and SDL); 193.3in (SEC); 199.2in (US-model SEC)
Wheelbase:	115.6in (SE); 121.2in (SDL and SDL); 112.2in (SEC)
Overall width:	71.5in
Unladen height:	56.5in (SE); 56.7in (SEL); 55.4in (SEC)
Track:	60.8in (front); 59.7in (rear)

Weights (typical)

260SE:	1508kg (3329lb)
420SE:	1598kg (3527lb)
500SEL:	1699kg (3751lb) (US model 1767kg/3900lb)
560SEC:	1748kg (3858lb)
560SEL:	1807kg (3990lb)

The S class was the Mercedes flagship, and as the 1990s opened it was the W126 range that filled the role. This is a standard-wheelbase saloon.

three V8 petrol engines, as 420SEC, 500SEC and 560SEC types.

By the turn of the decade, the W126 models were already quite long in the tooth. The saloons had been introduced at the Frankfurt Show in September 1979, and the coupés had followed two years later. There had been a mid-life facelift for both ranges in 1985, together with new engines, and in fact the cars had worn very well. However, the replacement W140s and C140s were already well into their development phase at Stuttgart, and the new saloons would go on sale in

October 1991 while the coupés would follow in January 1992. So there were no changes of any real significance to the W126 and C126 models after the start of the 1990s.

None of that prevented them from continuing to sell strongly and, as the replacement models met with a certain amount of market resistance in the beginning (*see* Chapter 4), resale values remained high for some years to come. Today, the C126 coupés – especially the 560SEC – are still viewed as among the most desirable Mercedes of the post-1945 era.

3   Personal Luxury

The R129 SL Roadsters

Mercedes-Benz has traditionally described the S class saloons as its flagship models, but it has never under-estimated the importance of its SL roadsters as image-bearers. Tracing their lineage back to the 300 SL Gullwing models of the 1950s, these cars have always symbolized a lifestyle based on wealth and personal freedom. To many people, they also represent the ultimate sports car, although since the 1960s the sporting element in their make-up has never been allowed to predominate over the personal-luxury element.

When the R129 SL range was introduced in 1989, the cars of the R107 range that it replaced were still selling strongly. Introduced in 1971, the R107 was by this stage hopelessly outdated, its chrome-laden styling quite clearly belonging to a different age. Yet it was still a desirable piece of property after 18 years in production, and by the time the last one rolled off the assembly lines, no fewer than 237,287 had been built. Of those, nearly 150,000 had gone to the USA – a powerful demonstration, if one were needed, of the importance of the US market to sales of the SL range. For the new SL, the US market would once again be a top priority.

In fact, work on the R107's replacement had begun in 1972, the year after the model had been introduced. The challenge of the Oil Crisis of 1973–1974 had then forced Stuttgart to allocate its design and engineering resources elsewhere, and work on the next-generation SL had not resumed until 1975. However, the

Like all Mercedes SLs, the R129 is perhaps most recognizable in open form. The projector-style headlamps and the spoked alloy wheels would mark this one out as a late example, even if the registration plate did not give the game away.

These 16-spoke alloy wheels were standard wear on early R129s, but other designs soon became available.

longer-term effects of that first Oil Crisis were still being felt, and as a result work on the new SL was again suspended while resources were devoted to a new compact saloon – the W201 or 190 range. Only when this car had been signed off for production could work begin once again on the new SL.

Right from the start, however, it had been clear that the new roadster would have to improve on its predecessor's already impressive array of safety features. In the early 1970s, there were fears within the motor industry that the US might outlaw open cars altogether on safety grounds, and such fears struck right at the heart of the SL concept. So a major part of the design brief was to make the new SL as safe in every kind of accident – and especially in a rollover – as a Mercedes-Benz saloon.

Early studies for the car that would become the R129 were quite radical. Some even proposed a mid-engined layout, although these were probably doomed from the start because the roadsters would have to share engines and drivetrain components with the S class and other saloons, which had a conventional rear-wheel-drive layout. Nevertheless, mid-mounted engines were still in the frame as late as 1979, and had probably not been finally ruled out until 1982. By that stage, work on the new car had become very much more focused – as indeed it needed to be. The R107 had by then been in production for 11 years and was already coming to the end of its anticipated design life. It was fortunate for Stuttgart that its sales continued to hold up so well, because the new SL was still several years away from production.

The appearance of the new car was once again the responsibility of Mercedes' styling chief Bruno Sacco, and his team had begun in the traditional fashion by producing a series of concept drawings. The most promising of these (between twelve and twenty in number, depending on who tells the story) were then selected to be turned into one-fifth-scale three-dimensional models. A choice was then made from these models, and again the most promising reached the next stage of the process: to be turned into full-size models made of wood, plastic and clay.

Throughout the design process, the styling proposals fell into three distinct groups. At one

37

ABOVE: *One characteristic of the R129 design was these side vents, which both provided a styling feature and recalled the side vents on the 300SL of the 1950s.*

LEFT: *Early cars had amber lenses for the turn indicators; later cars had smoked-glass lenses. The three-pointed star embedded in the grille was characteristic of the 'sports' Mercedes at this stage of the marque's evolution.*

extreme were the radical proposals and at the opposite extreme were the more conservative, which drew heavily on earlier SLs. The third group was of course a compromise between the two, and it was no real surprise that the design finally chosen in 1984 was one of these. Drawn up by Johann Tomforde, it married modern aerodynamics with styling touches that recalled the SL heritage.

Most striking, perhaps, was the wedge-shaped profile of the car, with a steeply raked windscreen and short tail. In marked contrast to the R107, the car had no exterior chrome, and its flanks were adorned with plastic protection panels, reflecting the style that Sacco had established for the entire Mercedes range of the early 1990s. Inset into these panels just behind the front wheel arches and giving character to the sides were air vents that deliberately recalled a feature of the original 300SL Gullwing. At the front, the traditional Mercedes 'sports' grille was flanked by rectangular headlamps and wraparound turn indicator lenses. Alloy wheels of the latest 16-spoke pattern were standard right across the range. It was, unmistakeably, an SL for the 1990s.

While Sacco's designers had been busy getting the shape right, another team at Stuttgart had been working on rollover safety. The threat of US legislation to outlaw open cars had now receded, and so the team's aim was simply to create the safest open car in the world. A targa-type roof was ruled out at an early stage, not least because such structures were already closely associated with rival manufacturer Porsche, and a fixed rollover bar was ruled out as reducing the aesthetic appeal of an open car. There was, then, only one option left, and this was to develop a system that would protect the occupants in a rollover but would remain invisible for the rest of the time. It took the Mercedes engineers nearly five years and £8.6 million to develop the system they wanted.

Electronics were becoming increasingly important in automotive design by the early 1980s, and it was electronics that provided the solution to the rollover safety problem. Stuttgart's revolutionary new concept depended on a rollover bar located behind the passenger compartment that would normally be concealed within the bodywork but would pop up when sensors indicated that a rollover was imminent. Deployment was rapid: the padded bar was spring-loaded and was in place within 0.3 seconds once the sensors and central control unit had agreed that it was needed. Thinking of everything (as was the Mercedes way), the engineers also provided for slower deployment by hydraulic rams, so that drivers of a nervous disposition could drive with the bar erect all the time. It could also be erected as a support for an optional wind blocker – in effect, a fabric mesh panel that reduced the amount of wind buffeting on the back of the occupants' heads at speed.

Despite this remarkable new piece of design and its streamlined appearance, the new R129 followed the established SL pattern. It was essentially a two-seater roadster with optional (and impractical) rear seats. In common with earlier SLs, it had a removable hard top – this time standard rather than an optional extra. Considerable design effort had gone into this, and no fewer than thirty-four different roof styles had been tried before the production style had been settled. Made of aluminium alloy, the hard top was some 10kg (22lb) lighter than its equivalent on the R107 models,

although it still needed two people to haul it on and off the car.

The soft top faithfully reflected the sleek lines of the hard top, and came with its own new technology. It was fully power-operated, and one touch of a large red button on the centre console was all that was needed. Aided by fifteen hydraulic pumps and seventeen micro-switches, the top would emerge from under its hinged metal tonneau cover behind the seats, the side windows would drop slightly, and the top would unfurl across the passenger compartment. As it locked into place automatically on the windscreen header rail, the windows would be raised again and the tonneau cover would close. The whole operation took fewer than 30 seconds – easily fast enough to be carried out while the car was stationary at traffic lights – and was just as simple and quick when the soft top was being stowed. A safety interlock ensured that the soft top could not be raised or lowered on the move.

In their rush to heap praise on this miracle of modern engineering, many commentators at the time overlooked the fact that Mercedes had been forced to make one compromise: the rear window was still a plastic item, when some rivals were already offering proper glass rear windows in their convertible tops.

A perennial problem with open cars was that the less than ideal aerodynamics caused wind buffeting at speed. To counter this, Mercedes introduced a wind blocker for the R129 models.

The soft top was a snug fit when erected, and its lines closely followed those of the removable hard top. The creases visible in the fabric of this one suggest it had not been erected for a long time before the picture was taken!

The removable hard top of the R129 models was carefully styled to blend in with the car's lines. As this picture of a 1992 model shows, it could be mistaken for an integral part of the car's body.

The rear end of the R129 incorporated characteristic Mercedes design features, such as the ribbed lenses on the lamp units.

Nevertheless, the sight of an SL opening up or closing down its soft top remains impressive even a decade and a half after the car was introduced.

Although the new SL was very roughly the same size as the car it replaced, it actually sat on a slightly longer wheelbase to provide more interior room. Overall length was increased by 7.5cm (3in), although in the USA the car was in fact shorter than the R107 because the latest safety-bumper design did away with the need for the horrible extended bumpers that had disfigured US versions of the R107; US and non-US versions of the R129 looked exactly the same. The car was also 2.5cm (1in) wider than its predecessor, with widened tracks. Above all, it was heavier – on average 90kg (200lb) heavier than the R107 and around 225kg (500lb) heavier than an equivalent-engined mid-range Mercedes saloon! Sporty it may have been to look at, but this weight made clear that the design emphasis had been on issues other than extreme agility and straight-line performance.

The extra weight was attributable partly to the complex soft-top and rollover bar systems, and partly to body reinforcement, which had been added both to maintain crash-safety levels and to prevent scuttle-shake. The latter had nearly ceased to exist thanks to a pair of profiled struts, each with its own vibration damper, which tied the front axle carrier to the door sills, plus two more tubular struts, which tied the sills to the spare wheel recess at the rear. Overall, Stuttgart claimed that the body shell of the R129 was 60 per cent stiffer than that of the R107 it replaced.

The Mercedes engineers had paid special attention to safety inside the passenger compartment, too. The seats were constructed with strong but lightweight magnesium frames that helped to protect their occupants from collision forces in a side impact. Seat belts were integral with the seats – which tilted to give access to the rear but were locked to the floor by Mercedes' tried and tested vacuum locking system when the engine was running – and their upper mountings were raised and low-

The fascia design of the R129 was typical Mercedes of its period, with five neat dials in a binnacle integrated into the sweep of the dashboard. This is an early example, built before the driver's airbag was standardized.

ered automatically along with the head restraints to give an ideal position. A driver's-side airbag was standard, while one for the passenger's side was also available.

New for the R129 was a variant of the traditional, clear Mercedes instrument layout with five dials instead of the three seen in the cars of the 1980s. However, it added no new driver information: the clock and fuel gauge had simply been removed from their combination dials and placed at the outer edges of the instrument panel. It looked good, but the rim of the steering wheel tended to obscure the outer two dials. The steering column itself was made adjustable for both reach and rake for the first time in a Mercedes, and of course power adjustment was on the menu; on some models, the steering wheel retracted automatically when the driver's door was opened, to make entry and exit easier.

Slated as an option on some models and as standard on others were power-adjusted seats with a position memory. This allowed a driver to re-set automatically seats, steering wheel, door mirrors and even the interior mirror (which was also power-operated) to his or her ideal position. A dust filter was fitted to the ventilation system, and an additional switch

activated a pump that circulated hot engine coolant through the heater for up to 30 minutes after the engine had been switched off, to keep a stationary car warm. Central locking was only to be expected, but on the SL all six interior compartments – including one for sunglasses in the centre of the dash and a map pocket in each door – could be locked, along with the doors and boot. This made the interior a more secure place to leave valuable items, especially if the car was parked with its top down.

Although the floor pan of the R129 had been purpose-designed, its suspension drew on existing Mercedes practice. At the front was a version of the strut suspension pioneered on the W201 compact saloons and the W124 mid-range cars, while at the rear was the acclaimed five-link layout familiar from the same models. On top of this, the R129 could be had with ADS damper control, which automatically adjusted the damper settings to suit the driving conditions and also lowered the ride height by 15mm (just over half an inch) above 120km/h (75mph) to improve stability. A manual control allowed the driver to raise the body for additional ground clearance at low speeds. The big disc brakes, ventilated at the front, came as standard with ABS. Also available was the linked ASR system, which backed off the power if it detected wheel spin. The ASD limited-slip differential could be ordered, too.

1989: The First Models

The new SL was introduced to the world at the Geneva Motor Show in March 1989, several months ahead of its showroom availability and also some months before full production began, in June. Yet there were already large numbers of R129s in existence: in addition to the mules and prototypes that had done the initial testing, Mercedes had assembled 1300 pilot-build cars. And, as the initial release of SLs reached the showrooms in the autumn of that year and (for right-hand-drive markets) the first few months of 1990, work was already going ahead on exciting developments, which would be revealed later.

There were three R129 models introduced for the 1990 model-year in autumn 1989. The entry-level car was the 300SL, powered by a version of the 190bhp 3-litre six-cylinder M103 engine already familiar from the W124 saloons, estates and coupés and from the W126

S class models. A new combustion chamber design and a different camshaft reduced exhaust emissions over earlier versions of this engine. The poverty-specification cars (if any SL deserves such a description) came with check cloth upholstery, a five-speed manual gearbox and a simple air-conditioning system. However, the options list exerted its usual fascination for most buyers, and leather upholstery, a four-speed automatic transmission and automatic temperature-controlled air conditioning probably featured on a majority of 300SLs. From October 1990 in Europe, the four-speed automatic was replaced by Mercedes' new W5A 030 five-speed overdrive type – the world's first volume-production five-speed automatic gearbox.

Next up in the pecking order was the 300SL-24, with the 231bhp 24-valve M104 engine, again with a 3-litre swept volume. Confusingly, this car was badged simply as a 300SL in the USA, which did not take the ordinary 300SL with its two-valve engine. The five-speed manual transmission was available on this car, too, although the four-speed automatic was much more popular and customers could order a five-speed close-ratio manual transmission with direct top gear and a slight-

Recognizably similar to the earlier design, the later R129 fascia had nevertheless evolved. Note the bright rings around the instrument dials and the steering wheel incorporating an airbag.

ly awkward dog's-leg shift pattern. The five-speed automatic became available on this model, too, and was in fact offered in the USA slightly earlier than in Europe.

Right at the top came the 500SL with 326bhp from its 5-litre V8 engine. The car marked the debut of the M119 V8 with its four-valve heads and variable cam timing, and was available only with the four-speed automatic transmission. It was a worthy range-topper, too: more than three seconds quicker to 60mph than a 300SL, it seemed to have endless reserves of torque to deliver smooth acceleration at all speeds right up to its electronically limited 250km/h (155mph) maximum. This speed had been settled by the agreement among Germany's car-makers to limit top speeds, but right from the start Mercedes were happy to point out that a de-restricted 500SL would be capable of 270km/h (170mph). No doubt several cars had their speed limiters disabled when eager owners wanted to prove this for themselves!

Press and customers alike were bowled over by the new cars, although there was no doubt that their great weight blunted their sporting edge or that the hood and rollover bar systems ate into the boot space. Some of the colour combinations resulting from Mercedes' inability to match the plastic flank panels to the main body colour were also distinctly questionable. Handling was vice-free, but a few journalists complained that the ASR system severely limited their fun by making it impossible to hang the tail out on corners. The customers mostly failed to understand what the journalists were talking about, however: they had no intention of driving like that themselves and were only too happy to have electronic systems to prevent over-exuberance getting them into trouble.

Waiting lists quickly built up. This was also the time of the great boom in cars as 'investments', and some shrewd individuals who had ordered early managed to off-load their new SLs at a good profit. In the UK, it was possible for a time in 1990 to sell a new 500SL at two and a half times the showroom price! However, when the Western economic boom turned to bust in 1991–1992, these options rapidly disappeared. The waiting lists, once measured in years, also shrank, and it soon became possible to go into a Mercedes show-room and buy a new SL more or less on the spot as long as colour and specification were not big issues. However, Stuttgart had already prepared a second wave of new models to protect residual values and bolster buyer interest in the SL range.

1993: New Names, New Models

This second wave of R129 models was not so much a wave as a tsunami: Stuttgart was determined not to allow the creeping recession to damage sales of its image-leader. While the 500SL remained in production, newly renamed the SL500 in line with the latest company policy, the 300SL gave way to a smaller-engined SL280 and the 300SL-24 gave way to a bigger-engined SL320. Right at the top of the range, the V12-engined SL600, which had been rumoured since the start of production, provided a new flagship for the 1994-season roadsters. Meanwhile, a passenger's-side airbag became standard on all models.

The SL280 of course had the 2.8-litre four-valve M104 engine with variable valve timing; with 197bhp, this was more powerful than the M103 3-litre single-cam straight-six that it replaced and delivered better acceleration, a higher top speed and better fuel economy into the bargain. The SL320 introduced the 3.2-litre four-valve M104, this time with no more power than the outgoing twin-cam 3-litre but with a better spread of torque to improve on the earlier engine's rather frenzied performance. Meanwhile, the SL500 had a modified engine-management system to improve exhaust emissions: full-load fuel enrichment was deleted, making a very slight improvement in fuel economy as well.

There was no doubt that the SL600 was a very special car, bringing all of six litres

Although there were V8s and even a V12 further up the range, the core engines of the R129 were six-cylinders. This is the M104 3.2-litre of an SL320.

(5987cc, to be precise) and 394bhp to the SL range. Some motoring writers nevertheless found it rather disappointing, not least because there was almost no aural indication that the V12 engine was accelerating the SL very rapidly indeed. The SL600 was also a much heavier car than the SL500, with an extra 150kg (330lb) to carry around. Stuttgart had done its best to maintain the handling balance, but the SL600 was noticeably heavier at the front than its V8 sibling, with a 53 per cent bias towards the front (the SL500 had a 52 per cent front bias and the two sixes were neatly balanced 50/50). This of course altered its handling characteristics slightly, and the impression of a nose-heavy car was reinforced by the extra 5-cm (2-in) depth of its front bumper – necessary to maintain crash-performance characteristics with the longer engine. It was a car for those who wanted the ultimate personal-luxury two-seater. Those who wanted the ultimate performance SL had to wait another year until the first AMG derivative was ready.

Like the V8 in the latest SL500, the M120 V12 engine in the SL600 did not have full-load fuel enrichment, and as a result it developed 13bhp less than its equivalent in the S class saloons. It also had a different sump and manifolding, a different air filter and a unique accessory drive. With the standard four-speed automatic transmission, Mercedes claimed that the SL600 would hit 60mph from rest in just under six seconds; indeed, the American *Car and Driver* magazine managed to record a 5.5-second time on test.

In most other respects, however, the SL600 was simply a very well-specified R129. Pretty well everything that was an optional extra on lesser models was standard on the car, although there were also two special distinguishing features: the discreet V12 badge positioned on each of the side air vents and some extra wood trim in the cabin.

1995–1998: Production Changes

During the middle 1990s, the SL280, SL320, SL500 and SL600 were joined by some formidably quick AMG-developed SLs, which are described below. But their own development did not stand still, and the 1996, 1997 and 1998 model-years brought a series of incremental changes.

The 1996 models arrived over the summer and autumn of 1995 and, as usual, the USA received the new season's models a month or so before most other countries. Keeping ahead of the opposition, the SL became available with side airbags, which were concealed behind the door trim cards. The design of these was correspondingly simplified, and the automatic locking of the map pockets was deleted. Out, too, went the power-operated interior mirror, while the climate control panel was given a bigger and more legible LCD screen.

On the outside, a subtle change to the air vents on the front wings left them with two inlets rather than three, and a slightly different shape as well. But most important for the best-selling SL500 was the arrival of the five-speed overdrive automatic gearbox already seen on the six-cylinder cars. The 5-litre V8 was also modified slightly, its power rising from 315bhp to 322bhp while maximum torque dropped from 345lb ft to 332lb ft.

The next season brought some attractive new wheel options, including a so-called Sport package, which consisted of 18in wheels with 8-in rims at the front and 9in rims at the rear. The associated tyres were 245/40ZR18s and 275/35ZR18s respectively. An automatic rain sensor for the windscreen wipers proved more

useful than its description suggested: drivers could leave the wipers on their 'intermittent' setting and let the electronics do the rest. There was also a new Panorama hard-top option with a full glass roof section, which was expensive enough to remain quite rare.

The 1997 season was the last one in the USA for the SL320, and for 1998 only the SL500 and SL600 were available there. The 1998 cars had a modified remote control for the central locking and alarm systems and a new LCD read-out panel on the dash, which included the new ASSYST service interval indicator.

The AMG SLs

Performance addicts had to wait until autumn 1994 for an ultra-high performance SL to become available through Mercedes showrooms. However, the SL60 AMG introduced for the 1995 model-year was not the tuning company's first brush with the R129. It was, in fact, a refinement of AMG's earlier 6-litre conversion for the 500SL. There had also been a 272bhp 3.4-litre derivative of the 300SL-24, which had been built in penny numbers, as had other aftermarket conversions by the likes of Brabus and Carlsson.

What made the SL60 AMG special was AMG's new agreement with Stuttgart. It had been possible to order AMG cars through Mercedes dealerships in earlier times, but now the increasingly close relationship between tuner and car-maker had led to something approaching official endorsement. There was no doubt that this reassured customers about such issues as service support and warranty cover, and there was equally no doubt that it helped sales of the AMG cars while adding lustre and some very exclusive models to the Mercedes range.

Despite its name, the SL60 was not a derivative of the SL600 but rather of the SL500. Its engine was an AMG-developed version of the 5-litre V8, bored out to 100mm to take the swept volume up to 5956cc. The tuned engine

Initially an independent concern specializing in high-performance Mercedes, AMG gradually grew closer and closer to Stuttgart until it was adopted as the performance arm of the company. The AMG badge on the boot lid of this R129 then became a mark of prestige as well as of performance.

AMG buyers demanded that their cars should look different from the regular production models, as well as go faster. This R129 features the AMG 'body kit' of special sills and front apron, plus AMG-designed wheels.

It is worth comparing the sills, wheels and front apron on this car with those on the AMG model (see above). The AMG items were not to every buyer's taste, but they did make the standard items look plain by comparison.

boasted 375bhp – 22 per cent more than its parent – and massive torque of 427lb ft at lower crankshaft speed than the parent engine generated its maximum 332lb ft. The paper figures show that this was going to be a very quick car, and so it proved: 60mph came up from rest in just 5.6 seconds, and the AMG SL just kept on accelerating all the way to its 250km/h (155mph) cut-out. Not only was it quicker than an SL600, but it was almost as smooth, and boasted the added attraction of a V8 exhaust soundtrack to excite the enthusiast driver.

The engine was harnessed initially to a four-speed automatic gearbox, but later models switched to the five-speed automatic when that became available on the 1996 model and later SL500s. The SL60 was fitted with distinctive AMG 18in alloy wheels, with 8in rims at the front and 9in rims at the rear wearing lower-profile tyres than on the standard SLs. Stiffer spring and damper rates made the ADS adaptive damping system superfluous, and the SL60 never had it. It was, though, distinguished by a special body kit of aprons and sills: buyers of this kind of car wanted more than just a badge on the boot lid to tell onlookers what they were looking at!

Of course, it was only to be expected that some buyers would insist on an ultra-high-performance SL with that stupendous V12 engine, and AMG had no intention of disap-

The SL was a delightful car to drive, especially with the top down. However, it was more of a tourer than a raw sporting car. This is a 2001 model.

pointing them. As a result, the SL60 AMG was joined after a year by an even more expensive SL73 AMG, a car which was destined to remain one of the rarest of all R129 SLs. Taken out of production after a few months, it was then put back into very limited production in 1998 and remained available until 2001, but the tiny numbers sold ensured that it would always remain an extreme rarity.

The engine that AMG developed for the SL73 was based on the M120 V12. Bored out to 91.5mm and stroked to 92.4mm with a new crankshaft, it had a swept volume of 7291cc. This delivered an astounding 525bhp, and of course drove through the latest five-speed

automatic gearbox. This was good enough for super-car maker Pagani to buy the engine for its C12S model (the C12 already used the standard M120 V12 engine), and in due course the engine would also appear in the CLK-DTR AMG racers.

The AMG V12's 553lb ft of torque were put down on the road through a special wheel-and-tyre combination with 9.5in rims at the rear. These were matched by 8.5in rims at the front. And, to ensure that customers really were getting a good deal for their money, AMG decided that they were not subject to the maximum-speed agreement among German manufacturers and omitted the speed limiter from

---

How Fast? How Thirsty?

These figures are typical for R129 SL models, but variations in the car's equipment levels and load, and variations in driving style will cause differences that may be significant.

	0–60mph	Max speed	Mpg (overall)
SL280	9.9sec	225km/h (140mph)	26 (10.8ltr/100km)
SL280 (V6)	9.5sec	227km/h (142mph)	23 (12.3ltr/100km)
300SL	9.5sec	220km/h (138mph)	24 (11.8ltr/100km)
300SL-24	8.4sec	230km/h (143mph)	24 (11.8ltr/100km)
SL320	8.4sec	238km/h (149mph)	26 (10.8ltr/100km)
SL320 (V6)	8.4sec	237km/h (148mph)	23 (12.3ltr/100km)
500SL/SL500	6.2sec	250km/h (155mph) (limited)	22 (12.8ltr/100km)
	(6.5sec from Sep 1992)		(20/14ltr/100km from Sep 1992)
600SL/SL600	6.1sec	250km/h (155mph) (limited)	18 (15.7ltr/100km)

This publicity picture of a 2001 SL320 was taken primarily to illustrate the appeal of the SL range, although it does show the car's sleek lines rather well, too!

the engine-management system. As a result, the SL73 AMG had a maximum speed of around 290km/h (185mph) and devoured the 0–60mph segment in just 4.8 seconds.

However, the new and closer relationship with Stuttgart meant that AMG needed to develop engines that would suit a wide range of cars, and the most cost-effective way of doing this was to focus on one engine at a time. The SL60 AMG with its 6-litre V8 was withdrawn at the end of the 1997 model-year, and in its place for 1998 came an SL55 AMG with the tuning company's version of the brand-new three-valve V8. With capacity raised from 5 litres to the 5.5-litres its name suggested (actually 5439cc), this delivered 349bhp – noticeably down on the SL60 AMG's 375bhp. While the 0–60mph time was only 0.3 seconds slower and the SL55 was limited to the same 250km/h (155mph) maximum speed as its predecessor had been, these differences mattered to many of those who were wealthy enough to own an AMG-developed SL. The fact that the new 5.5-litre engine was far more refined and fuel-efficient than the earlier AMG V8 was probably lost on many of them.

This, then, was almost certainly the reason why the SL73 AMG reappeared as a 1999 model alongside the new SL55 AMG. Those who wanted the absolute maximum performance were thus able to buy a faster car than the outgoing SL60 AMG, while the new SL55

AMG catered for the rest and its greater availability undoubtedly brought new owners into the AMG fold. Making the SL73 AMG available once again was no big problem for AMG, as its engine had remained in low-volume production for the Pagani C12S. Besides, it was destined to remain such a rare car that hand-building a few extra engines can hardly have been a major hardship!

Best Buys

Various factors can influence purchase costs from time to time, and it is not possible to take these into account here. However, in terms of practicality and enjoyment, these are the best R129 SL models to buy.

Although the top-of-the-range models were V8s and V12s, these can be expensive to own. There is absolutely no shame in going for one of the six-cylinder cars, although it is worth remembering that many of these were built without some of the desirable options that were standard on the bigger-engined models. If fuel economy is an important issue, it is worth noting that the V6 (and later three-valve V8) cars are generally less thirsty than their earlier equivalents.

A best buy? The middle-of-the-range 300SL-24 and SL320 six-cylinder models are a good bet, although there is no denying the appeal of the 5-litre V8 option.

The Final Years

The big news in 1998, however, affected the mainstream SL models. To carry the range through until its replacement R230 was ready in mid-2001, Mercedes gave the SLs a facelift and a pair of new engines. At the same time, the range was reduced from four models to three, as the SL280 went out of production.

The facelift brought the cars more into line with the latest styling changes elsewhere in the Mercedes line-up. The exterior door handles were now painted to match the body-work and the original ribbed tail-light lenses disappeared in favour of a smoother design with more rounded contours. Inside the car, the five instrument dials were ringed in silver, an oil-temperature gauge replaced the oil-pressure gauge, and a new steering wheel with a more consciously styled centre section was standardized.

The new engines were the very latest 'modular' vee types, a V6 for the new SL320 and a V8 for the new SL500. Confusingly, their swept volumes were the same as those of the engines they replaced – 3199cc for the V6 and 4973cc for the V8 – but both had the new three-valve layout and delivered lower exhaust emissions and better fuel economy. Both also had the benefit of improved bottom-end torque, and both came with the five-speed automatic transmission. Maximum power was down on the engines they replaced, but their other undoubted benefits made this of little consequence.

Thus modified, the R129 models remained essentially unchanged until production ended in 2001. Their final months were marked by a commemorative edition, called the Silver Arrow and based on the SL500. In the UK, there were just 100 of these cars, each one numbered and sold with a certificate of authenticity signed by Stirling Moss, the man who had piloted a 300SLR to victory in the 1955 Mille Miglia. The cars were all silver, with a special badge and six-spoke 18-in alloy wheels. The interior was upholstered in black and white leather while its wood trim was black bird's-eye maple, and the ensemble was completed by the rare Panorama glass-roofed hard top.

Later cars had a third brake light embedded in the boot lid. Compare the rear view of this SL500 with the rear view of the blue earlier car on page 41.

Specifications for R129 Models

Engines

SL280	2799cc M104 6-cyl, 193PS & 270Nm	(1993–1998)
	2799cc M112 V6, 204PS & 270Nm	(1998–2001)
300SL	2962cc M103 6-cyl, 190PS & 260Nm	(1989–1993)
300SL-24	2962cc M104 6-cyl, 231PS & 272Nm	(1989–1993)
SL320	3199cc M104 6-cyl, 231PS & 315Nm	(1993–1998)
	3199cc M112 V6, 224PS & 315Nm	(1998–2001)
500SL	4973cc M119 V8, 326PS & 450Nm	(1989–1992)
	4973cc M119 V8, 320PS & 470Nm	(1992–1993)
SL500	4973cc M119 V8, 320PS & 470Nm	(1993–1998)
	4966cc M113 V8, 306PS & 460Nm	(1998–2001)
SL55 AMG	5439cc M113 V8, 354PS & 530Nm	(1999–2001)
AMG 500SL 6.0	5956cc M119 V8, 374PS & 550Nm	(1991–1993)
SL60 AMG	5956cc M119 V8, 381PS & 580Nm	(1993–1998)
600SL	5987cc M120 V12, 394PS & 570Nm	(1992–1993)
SL600	5987cc M120 V12, 394PS & 570Nm	(1993–2001)
SL73 AMG	7291cc M120 V12, 525PS & 750Nm	(1999–2001)

Transmissions

Five-speed manual
Four-speed automatic (to Sep 1995)
Five-speed automatic (from Sep 1995)

Running gear

Front suspension with wishbones and struts; self-levelling optional; anti-roll bar and variable dampers on 600SL/SL600.

Multi-link rear suspension with coil springs, telescopic dampers and anti-roll bar; variable dampers on 600SL/SL600.

Power-assisted recirculating-ball steering.

Power-assisted brakes with ABS as standard; Brake Assist on 600SL/SL600; ventilated front disc brakes; solid rear disc brakes to Aug 1993 (except on 600SL/SL600); ventilated rear discs from Sep 1993 (and on all 600SL/SL600 models).

Weights (typical)

SL280:	2150kg (4730lb)
SL280 (V6):	2130kg (4686lb)
300SL (to Aug 1991):	2040kg (4488lb)
300SL (from Sep 1991):	2080kg (4576lb)
300SL-24 (to Aug 1991):	2080kg (4576lb)
300SL-24 (from Sep 1991):	2130kg (4686lb)
SL320:	2170kg (4774lb)
SL320 (V6):	2130kg (4686lb)
500SL (to Sep 1991):	2160kg (4752lb)
500SL (from Sep 1991 to Aug 1995):	2190kg (4818lb)
SL500 (Sep 1995 to June 1998):	2230kg (4906lb)
SL500 (with M113 V8):	2210kg (4862lb)
SL55 AMG:	2210kg (4862lb)
SL600:	2320kg (5104lb)
SL60 AMG:	2230kg (4906lb)
SL73 AMG:	2320kg (5104lb)

Dimensions

Overall length:	4470mm (176in)
Wheelbase:	2515mm (99in)
Overall width:	1812mm (71in)
Overall height:	1293mm (51in) with hard top;
	1305mm (51in) with soft top
Track:	1535mm (60.5in) (front);
	1523mm (60in) (rear)

4 Flagship Saloons and Coupés

The 140 Models, 1991–1998

The story of the W140 saloons and related C140 coupé models is a fascinating one, not least because these were the first cars in the post-1945 history of the Mercedes-Benz marque to be received with less than total enthusiasm. In the early days of their existence, there were stories of vast stockpiles of unsold cars, and within a few years Stuttgart was frantically making revisions to keep the cars saleable. Even today, they divide opinions: to some, they epitomize the technological supremacy of Mercedes, while to others they are large and ugly irrelevancies.

So what went wrong? The previous range of S class cars (the W126s) had sold enormously well, to the tune of 890,000 in 11 years, and production ended on a high note in 1991. With the reputation of the S class at an all-time high, it seems barely credible that Mercedes could have got it wrong – but they did. What happened was that the W140 models were conceived at a time of economic boom in the Western world and their design was strongly influenced by the perceptions of those times. They looked big, even bloated, and they boasted unashamedly of their owners' wealth. Originally scheduled for introduction at the end of the 1980s, when they would have been perfectly in tune with their times, they suffered from a change of heart – some suggest a panic – at Stuttgart over the winter of 1985–1986.

The cause of this change of heart has never been publicly acknowledged, but it was almost certainly Mercedes' discovery that the new

Although the W140 has not won the hearts of Mercedes enthusiasts everywhere, examples do turn up at club events such as this one held in the UK.

This UK press picture shows an early S280 saloon, the entry-level model of the W140 range. Within the S class, however, even the entry-level model was a well-equipped, luxurious and prestigious car.

BMW 7 Series – due in 1987 and a direct competitor for the S class – was to have a V12 engine option. Jaguar, a smaller threat but one that was gradually getting stronger, already had such an engine in production. Recognizing that the S class would have to have its own V12 if it was not to look like a poor relation to BMW and Jaguar, Stuttgart set a development programme in motion and delayed the planned launch of the W140 until the new engine was ready. That delay meant that the new S class did not arrive until the economic boom of the late 1980s had turned to bust. The cars seemed inappropriate for the new economic conditions; the customers stayed away; and Stuttgart had to fight desperately hard to get them back.

Design

The proud and imposing styling that characterized the W140s was the work of Bruno Sacco's styling department, although there is some evidence that Sacco himself was not

Designer Bruno Sacco stands proudly alongside the S500 model that introduced the W140 to the world at the Geneva Show in 1991. Note the rather aggressive 'egg-crate' grille, which was not carried over to production cars.

wholly satisfied with the end result. Like so many cars, the new S class had to be styled around a tightly defined dimensional package, and the sheer size of this package gave the stylists some problems. One of their greater achievements was that the W140 looked smaller than it really was: this was, after all, a car that stood nearly 150cm (60in) tall and was actually taller than the contemporary Rolls-Royce Silver Spirit. It was also wider and longer than the W126 range that it replaced – and yet its drag co-efficient of just 0.31 was another astonishing achievement.

Some of the basic styling concepts reflected in the W140 had been established during the 1980s. Notable among these were the plastic flank protection panels, which had been pioneered on the W201 190E 2.3-16 in 1983. The W140 had the same angled sides to the boot opening, which had been so much liked on the W124s, and of course it shared a headlamp and tail-lamp style that was by the early 1990s very recognizably Mercedes.

And yet, as the flagship of the Mercedes line-up, it also had to incorporate a glimpse of the future. This it did in the so-called 'integrated' grille, which did away with the wide bright-metal frame that had characterized the Mercedes saloon grille for more than 60 years. The new grille was set into the metal of the bonnet panel, with the three-pointed star emblem standing a little way back. It was a design that would be adopted for other Mercedes models as the 1990s went on. Interestingly enough, the production design had probably not been settled until around the middle of 1991: the pre-production W140 that appeared at the Geneva Motor Show in early 1991 had a more ornate version of the grille, with bright horizontal as well as vertical bars.

The sheer size of the car had called for some compromises in the styling. Most of these were well disguised, but others remained uncomfortably visible. The absence of a continuous waistline was one compromise: the heights of front and rear wings had been fixed by the volumes of the boot and engine compartment,

Despite the elegant styling, even the alloy wheel of this V12-engined S600 looks big and heavy.

and so to avoid unduly small windows it had been necessary to enlarge them downwards. This also reduced the height of the doors' lower panels, which was no bad thing. However, the flanks of the car still looked flat and lacking in character. Thick roof pillars were in keeping with the generally bulky overall appearance, but they did restrict vision out of the car to some extent.

The body shell was of course a monocoque, but the front and rear suspension units were carried on sub-frames. This was mainly to provide better insulation of the cabin from road noise, but the front sub-frame was also carefully mounted so that in a collision it would act as a protective barrier against intrusion into the footwells. The suspension design was broadly similar to that on the W210 and W124 ranges, but had of course been adjusted to suit the characteristics of this larger and much heavier car. So the twin-wishbone front suspension incorporated a greater degree of anti-dive, while the five-link rear suspension had been redesigned to incorporate more anti-squat. It also had redesigned upper links which crossed one another diagonally, thus allowing

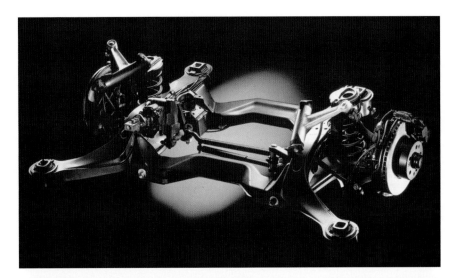

Marvellously dramatic publicity photograph showing the front sub-frame and suspension of the W140 series.

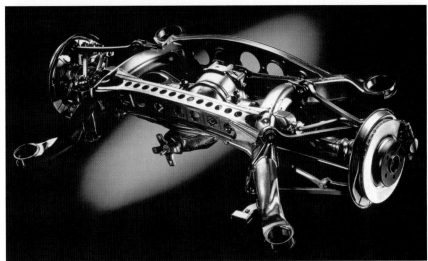

No expense spared: the complex rear suspension unit of a W140 S class car. It incorporated all the best of Mercedes' thinking on ride comfort and handling at the time.

the longer links that the W140 needed, while maintaining the compactness of the original design.

Stuttgart's engineers designed three types of suspension for the W140. Entry-level models had coil springs all round, with gas-pressure dampers. Next up in the pecking order came coil springs with a self-levelling rear suspension that maintained a constant ride height at the back even when the car was heavily loaded. This could be supplemented optionally by the ADS adjustable damping package,

which improved the ride quality. Top of the range was hydro-pneumatic suspension with ADS. This not only provided a superb ride, but was also programmed to lower the body at speeds above 120km/h (75mph), to improve stability. In addition, it could be manually over-ridden to raise the body by 20mm (just under an inch) at speeds below 80km/h (50mph) in order to provide more ground clearance over rough surfaces.

These were very heavy cars – thanks partly to their size and partly to the wealth of

An American publicity picture dating from 1998, probably intended to demonstrate that the W140 saloons had much better handling than their appearance suggested.

technological gadgetry they carried – so all models except the entry-level six-cylinders had ventilated disc brakes on all four wheels, supplemented of course by a servo and ABS. The entry-level cars had solid discs on the rear with ventilated discs at the front. An optional upgrade on some models was a brake pressure distribution system, which worked on the

The W140 S class was among the first cars in the world to be made available with a satellite navigation system. By today's standards, this early installation appears quite crude.

back of the ABS and ensured that optimum braking was available for all circumstances. This was, of course, standard on the top W140s. As for steering, the usual power-assisted recirculating-ball type was chosen once again, this time with some sophisticated modifications. The W140s had what Mercedes called 'parameter' steering, which varied the amount of power assistance provided in accordance with the road speed.

Right from the start, Mercedes had intended that the latest S class should have a wealth of on-board technology to demonstrate its superiority over rival models. As a result, it came with the very latest automatic air-conditioning system, a satnav system concealed in a dashboard compartment just above the centre air vents, electric motors to close its heavy doors over the last half-inch of their travel, and guide rods that popped up from the rear wings when Reverse was selected and allowed the driver to position the car more accurately. There was also a data bus linking the various control modules on the engine, gearbox, braking and traction control systems. This was still world-leading technology, even though it had already been seen on the small-volume 500E high-performance W124 saloon introduced just a year earlier.

Stuttgart was undoubtedly very proud of the fact that it had designed its new flagship with end-of-life disposal firmly in mind. The W140 was entirely free of CFCs, the chloro-fluoro-carbons believed to contribute to global warming. Each one of its plastic components also carried clear identification markings which would simplify recycling, and many of the components were in fact made from regranulated plastic. No doubt part of the impetus for all this had come from the increasingly powerful Green political party in Germany, but it would go down well in other countries, too. In 1992 – at a time when it needed all the praise it could get – the W140 won the Stratospheric Ozone Protection Award from the US Environmental Protection Agency.

However, the biggest news was double-glazing for the door windows – a world first that ultimately proved to be a dead end. Each door window consisted of two panes of 3mm glass separated by a 1mm air gap, and this innovation proved extremely effective at keeping noise out of the passenger cabin and at reducing the effect of outside temperature changes.

Double-glazed door windows reduced noise inside the cabin, but they were the kind of expensive refinement that Mercedes would consider an unnecessary complication by the end of the 1990s.

The interior of one of these cars incorporated more luxury than most buyers would have imagined possible. It was vastly more accommodating than even the W126 cabin had been, being a full 5.5in wider (although the car was actually just 2.6in wider overall

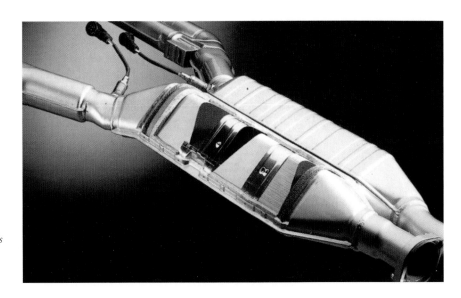

Emissions regulations of course affected the design of all Mercedes cars in this era. This is the exhaust catalyst of an early V12-engined W140.

than its predecessor). The seats were broad and widely spaced one from another. The sides of the console on the transmission tunnel at the front were upholstered in leather and there was a corresponding centre console between the rear seats – another idea pioneered on the W124 500E in 1990. As in the R129 roadsters, the steering column could be adjusted for both reach and for rake, and power assistance for both functions was available. The front seats came with power adjustment as standard, plus a programmable three-position memory that also covered the steering column when the adjustment for that was power-assisted.

Leather upholstery was of course standard, matched by more wood trim than had been seen in any other Mercedes saloon, and the dashboard and console carried a simply huge array of switches. These took some time for a new driver to learn, although they were in fact very logically laid out – in typical Mercedes fashion. Other notable features were the five-dial instrument pack that had been introduced on the R129 SLs in 1989 and a new and more compact airbag design, which permitted a neater steering wheel hub and allowed room

for a glove-box on the passenger's side of the dashboard.

Such safety features were perhaps only to be expected on a Mercedes, but the W140 went beyond what others had achieved. In addition to the standard airbag complement, there were pre-tensioners on the safety-belts, which allowed them more slack and therefore greater comfort in normal use. In addition, the already massively strong structure had been designed to meet and exceed the requirements of the new US side-impact legislation that would be introduced in 1994.

The First Models

The initial release of W140s in October 1991 consisted of no fewer than ten basic models. The entry-level car was the 300SE, with a 231bhp six-cylinder petrol engine. For some markets, which initially included the USA but never included the UK, there was also a 350SD with a 150bhp six-cylinder turbodiesel. Next up came the 400SE with a 218bhp petrol V8 and a 500SE with a 308bhp V8. Right at the top of the range came a 600SE powered by

The cabin of a W140 S class offered acres of space, and its ambience was perfectly suited to the requirements of the typical owner.

At the core of the 140 range were V8 engines, available in 4.2-litre and 5-litre forms.

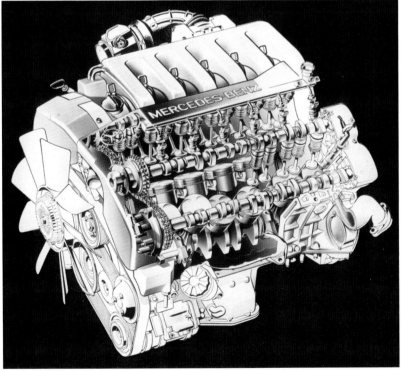

Everything looks straightforward under the bonnet, but pity the poor mechanic who has to work on one of these! The cutaway drawing shows the complexity of the 6-litre V12 engine.

This is the under-bonnet view of a right-hand-drive V12-engined W140. Mercedes' presentation of the engine was faultless, although these early V12s can be very expensive to maintain when they reach high mileages and old age.

Mercedes' brand-new advanced V12 petrol engine boasting 389bhp. Each one of these could also be had as a long-wheelbase model with an extra 100mm (4in) of length in the rear of the passenger cabin, becoming the 300SEL, 350SDL, 400SEL, 500SEL and 600SEL respectively.

Interestingly, the designations of the petrol models did not all match their engine sizes but were intended to give an indication of the range hierarchy. The engine of the 300SE actually had a swept volume of 3.2 litres (and in the USA it was actually badged as a 300SE 3.2), while that of the 400SE was a 4.2-litre. Only the 500SE with its 4973cc V8 and the 600SE with its 5987cc V12 were somewhere near the mark.

Every one of the new petrol engines was a four-valve design with variable timing on the inlet camshaft (or both inlet camshafts in the case of the V8s and V12). The entry-level six-cylinder was the latest version of the twin-cam M104 engine, while the two V8s both belonged to the M119 family. The all-new V12, meanwhile, carried the new designation of M120. As for the diesel, this was the latest version of the OM603 six-cylinder turbocharged and intercooled engine that had powered diesel derivatives of the outgoing W126 saloons.

Only the entry-level 300SE was available with a manual transmission, which was the GL76/30 B-5 close-ratio, direct-top type that was also mated to the M104 engine in the 300SL-24. Because of its nature, though, the 300SE was more commonly ordered with the alternative five-speed W5A 030 automatic. At this stage, however, the six-cylinder petrol models were the only ones which had the latest five-speed transmission: the V8s and V12 always had a four-speed automatic. This was the familiar W4A 040 type with the V8s and the stronger W4A 055 variety with the twelve-cylinder engine.

Just two types of wheel were available on these first models, both 16-in alloy designs with a 7.5-in rim width. Six-cylinder cars came as standard with a discreet style that had fifteen holes in its outer circumference; similar to the fifteen-hole alloys available since the mid-1980s on other models, these were nevertheless distinctively different because their centres were raised rather than dished. The optional alternative (which was standard on some models in some countries) was a new eight-hole design, which was supposedly more sporty. By all accounts, Bruno Sacco was none too happy to see these fitted to the S class, as he believed they detracted from its essential dignity! Tyres on the six-cylinder models were 225/60s, but wider 235/60s were fitted to all the V8s and the V12.

Nobody who viewed or evaluated the W140 when it first appeared was in any doubt that Stuttgart's engineers had excelled them-selves once again: the car was a technological *tour de force*, which had been designed with typical Mercedes thoroughness and was built to the usual impeccable standards. But right from the start, there was a feeling that this was a car that was not right for its times. It was too big, too plush and too much a product of the booming 1980s at a time when world economies were beginning to show a marked downturn. So the W140 got off to a bad start. It was grudgingly accepted as the new flagship Mercedes, but did not attract the sales that its makers had been hoping for.

By the end of 1991, it was clear that the Mercedes marque had a problem on its hands. Major redevelopment of the car to suit the mood of the times was out of the question: it would take too long and would be too costly. Some programmes for future development were already too advanced to be held back or altered. Among these were the development of big coupés based on the S class platform, which were due to be announced early in 1992 and to enter production that autumn. There were also armoured 500SE and 600SE variants, scheduled for introduction in February 1992.

Stuttgart probably did not wait for customer reactions before starting on a programme of making the saloons look smaller than they were. However, such changes could not be made overnight, and it would be two more years before the revised models reached the showrooms. Competitors rubbed their hands with glee at Stuttgart's discomfiture and quick-ly made inroads into the traditional customer base of the S class. Hindsight leaves no room for doubt that the initial problems of the W140 were a major factor in the blood-letting at

The V12 engine was fitted into the long-wheelbase saloon shell to produce the flagship model W140. Note the discreet but unmissable V12 badge on the rear pillar. The long-wheelbase cars always seemed better proportioned than the standard-wheelbase saloons.

board level, and in the re-thinking of engineering and model strategies that occurred in
the Mercedes car division in spring 1993.

Urgent Measures

Some kind of downsizing was obviously called
for, and by the time of the Paris Motor Show
in October 1992 Stuttgart was ready with new
models that were a clear statement of intent.

Most obvious was the introduction of a new
entry-level model called the 280SE (or 300SE
2.8 in the USA), which brought a short-stroke
version of the M104 six-cylinder engine. With
193bhp, it was considerably less powerful than
the 3.2-litre 300SE and it is doubtful whether
fuel economy was any better. However, it did
appeal to those who were worried about being
accused of conspicuous consumption, and it
went on to be a steady seller.

Continental European markets also benefited from the arrival of their own diesel model.
This was in fact pretty well identical with the
350SD that had been introduced a year earlier
for the USA but, tellingly, it was badged as a
300SD for Europe. Perceived engine size was
clearly one of the factors deterring customers,
and Stuttgart's marketing department had
responded to this. However, the diesel model
was not made available in the UK, where there
was still considerable resistance to diesel power
in general and where the idea of a diesel luxury saloon was still almost unthinkable.

There were improvements to the big-
engined 500SE and 600SE models, too, and of
course these also affected their long-wheelbase
derivatives. To improve fuel consumption (and
so to demonstrate to the buying public that
Stuttgart was thinking along the right lines),
both engines had their control modules modified to eliminate full-load fuel enrichment.
Maximum power dropped slightly in consequence, but, as both engines were electronically restricted to deliver no more than 250km/h
(155mph), actual performance did not suffer
noticeably. No similar change was made to the
S420, probably because the loss of maximum

*As introduced, the W140 models had amber lenses for the
indicator segments of the rear light units.*

speed would have been more obvious: the
S420 peaked at 243km/h (152mph) and had
no need of a limiter.

The next changes came early for the 1994
model-year, and were announced in June
1993. The most noticeable change, however,
was not one that affected customer perceptions of the S class image; in accordance with
the new Mercedes system, the W140s were rebadged. The name of every W140 saloon was
now prefixed with an S as the class identifier,
and there was no longer a letter to distinguish
long- and short-wheelbase models with the
same engine. Starting at the bottom, the 280SE
became an S280. Next up, the 300SE and
300SEL both became S320s, the new designation being a more accurate reflection of their
engine size. The old 300SD (350SD in the
USA) became an S350 Turbodiesel, while the
400SE became a more honest 420SE, and the
500SE and 600SE became S500 and S600
models respectively.

There were some obvious anomalies in this renaming system. If big engines had been deterring customers, why had the 300SE been clearly identified as having an apparently larger 3.2-litre engine, and the 400SE as an apparently larger 4.2-litre engine? Why had the 300SD become an apparently bigger-engined S350 Turbodiesel in Europe? The answer, almost certainly, was that Stuttgart was anticipating the new BMW 7 Series, which would arrive a year later. The Munich company had had time to learn from the W140's mistakes and would no doubt put up a formidable opponent. If BMW badged its cars to make them look as if they had bigger – and, by implication, more powerful – engines than the Mercedes, it would be another blow to the W140's fortunes. So the June 1993 renaming took pre-emptive action. Customers who did not want to let the world know the size of the engine in their W140 could always request them to be delivered without model badges.

The June 1993 changes also brought improvements in fuel economy for the S320 models. Claimed to be as high as 7.5 per cent, these improvements were brought about by the introduction of a variable-resonance inlet manifold and a hot-film air mass sensor in place of the earlier hot-wire type. Introduced in the W124 mid-range models at the same time, they brought increases in power and torque, while changes elsewhere in the engines resulted in lower friction losses. Clearly, Mercedes was still aiming to make every little improvement it could to improve the image and sales of the W140s.

Restyled

The new BMW 7 Series was expected in the autumn of 1994, and Stuttgart had probably always planned to upgrade its W140 range in some way to counter this new threat to sales. However, the nature of the upgrades that actually entered production was undoubtedly affected to a massive extent by the negative buyer reactions to the first W140s. So at the

These are the later rear light units, with smoked indicator lenses; compare them with the earlier type pictured on an S280. This view of an S600 also illustrates the way Mercedes integrated its parking sensors into the rear of the car.

Geneva Motor Show in February 1994, the revised S class was presented as a slimmer, leaner car. Bruno Sacco's stylists had done a great job in record time.

In truth, the cars were no smaller than before, but they certainly looked trimmer. The bottom edges of the sills and bumper aprons had been rolled under to reduce their apparent depth and so the apparent height of the body. The rear end's apparent height had meanwhile been reduced by a reflective band, which ran the full width of the car underneath the tail lamps and the boot lid. The lower corners of the boot lid had also been rounded off, using a design similar to that on the W140 coupés. These two changes helped draw attention to the car's width rather than its height.

At the front, the vertical bar separating dipped and main-beam elements of the headlamps had been suppressed, and the grilles on the sixes and the V8s had been slimmed down and given more of a peak in the centre. These two changes reduced the apparent bulk of the front end. By contrast, the V12 models took on a broader chrome frame for the grille, with chrome slats; this did not make the cars look any smaller, but presumably V12 buyers did not care what other people thought of their purchases, and were only too pleased to have them visually distinguished from lesser W140s!

There were also changes to the lamps front and rear for these 1995-season cars. Headlamps on all models were given optimized variable-focus reflectors, which increased their light output by 60 per cent. Clear indicator lenses with amber-tinted bulbs followed the latest trend, while bichromatic rear-light lenses removed some of the fussiness of the earlier types with their amber indicator segments.

Mercedes had of course kept some options up their sleeve so that they could respond quickly to the challenge of the new BMWs if there was a need. The new option of Parktronic distance-sensing radar for both front and rear was introduced in May 1995. Standard on S600 models, this replaced the guide rods that had risen from the rear wings on earlier cars.

The Final Three Seasons

The production life of the W140s was far from over by this stage, but there can be little doubt that Stuttgart did not even contemplate stretching it beyond the seven or eight years which had originally been planned. The new BMW had indeed proved to be a formidable threat, and its sleeker, lower lines were already making the S class look old and frumpy. Work on the replacement W220s had begun very soon after the W140s had gone on sale, and their introduction could not come a moment too soon.

The 1996 models were introduced at the Frankfurt Motor Show in September 1995 and featured largely incremental improvements. Fuel economy and emissions concerns were addressed in the V8 models by a new crankshaft, an improved variable valve timing system, lighter pistons, and a new Bosch Motronic management system featuring the hot-film air mass sensor seen earlier on the six-cylinder engines. A new ignition system provided one coil for each cylinder, to give better control of spark timing and duration. The arrangement of the V12's ignition coils was also changed, and this engine had its own modified management system.

Both the V8s and the V12s also took on the very latest electronically controlled five-speed automatic transmission in place of their older, hydraulically controlled four-speeds. Both transmissions were 'adaptive' types, which 'learned' the driver's style and adjusted change-up points to suit, and both also had a lock-up clutch in top gear. This combined with the engine changes to improve fuel economy by an average of 7 per cent across the board, while noxious emissions went down by a huge 40 per cent.

Also new for the 1996 W140s was the ESP electronic stability programme, which became optional for the V8 models but was made standard on the V12s. But the most interesting novelty at Frankfurt was the introduction of a new model called the S600 Pullman.

The S600 Pullman was announced nearly a year ahead of its actual availability, which began in August 1996, but Mercedes used it as a demonstration of superiority in the war against BMW. Known to Stuttgart as a V140 model (the V standing for *verlängert*, or 'lengthened'), it was a full metre longer than the existing long-wheelbase S600 model and had an extra window and accompanying lower body panel between the front and rear doors. In the extra space were fitted rearward-facing seats, so that the back of the car became a very comfortable cabin for four passengers. An optional glass division separated this compartment from the driving compartment, and those lucky enough to sit in the back could benefit from a vast array of extras designed to make life easy for the tycoon on the move.

However, sheer size was not the whole story. The S600 Pullman shown at Frankfurt also showcased new 'protection technology', as Mercedes called it. In other words, it was armoured to the very latest standards and incorporated features that had not been available as recently as 1992, when the first armoured W140s had been announced. The Pullman stretch was also made available without the armour plating on both S500 and S600 models, but this was inevitably a car that always remained a rare, bespoke and extremely expensive model.

The 1997 changes arrived in June 1996 and were once again incremental for the most part. However, they also brought a new and more powerful OM606 engine for the diesel W140, which was renamed an S300 Turbodiesel. This incorporated the latest four-valve technology, a turbocharger and an intercooler, and was harnessed to the latest five-speed transmission. With 177bhp, it had 27bhp more than the outgoing engine despite half a litre less swept volume, and although peak torque was up by only 14lb ft, torque delivery across the engine's speed range was very much more impressive.

All W140s had an exterior makeover, which left the exterior plastic panels in body colour rather than in the contrasting colour used on earlier cars. Front side airbags were standardized across the range, with a seat occupant sensor for the passenger's side, which prevented both side and front airbags being triggered (with the consequent high replacement cost) if the seat was not occupied. Luggage nets were also added in the boot and the passenger's-side footwell, and the latest show of technology involved rain-sensing windscreen wipers. A new option was Xenon headlamps with a wash-wipe and dynamic range adjustment.

Meanwhile, the six-cylinders also benefited from some mechanical changes. The five-speed automatic finally became standard on the S320, although it remained an option for the S280, and ASR was standardized on both models. A few months later, in December 1996, the sixes also took on ESP as standard, although not if they were fitted with the manual gearbox (by now rare). The W140 was also used to promote the introduction of the latest Brake Assist system, which automatically sensed an emergency stop and applied full braking power more quickly than a driver could manage.

The W140 saloons finally bowed out in summer 1998, when their successors, the

---

How Fast? How Thirsty?

These figures are typical for W140 S class models, but variations in the car's equipment levels and load, and variations in driving style will cause differences that may be significant.

	0–60mph	Max speed	Mpg (overall)
S300 Turbodiesel	11.2 secs	205km/h (128mph)	30 (9.4 ltr/100km)
S350 Turbodiesel	13.1 secs	185km/h (115mph)	25 (11.3 ltr/100km)
S280	11.0 secs	208km/h (130mph)	23 (12.3 ltr/100km)
S320	8.9 secs	225km/h (140mph)	24 (11.8 ltr/100km)
S420	8.3 secs	243km/h (152mph)	25 (11.3 ltr/100km)
S500	7.3 secs	250km/h (155mph) (limited)	22 (12.8 ltr/100km)
S600	6.6 secs	250km/h (155mph) (limited)	19 (31.4 ltr/100km)

Note: These figures are for standard-wheelbase saloons. Coupé models accelerate to 62 mph slightly more slowly and can be thirstier, especially in town traffic. Long-wheelbase models may also be thirstier.

W220s, were introduced. By that date, a total of 406,532 cars had been built in just seven seasons – an average of just over 58,000 a year. There had been 28,101 diesel-powered models. These totals may have been inflated slightly by a small number of cars – such as Pullman limousines and armoured variants – which were still in build at the time the assembly lines were closed in Stuttgart. But it was a deeply disappointing total compared to the 88,000 a year achieved by the W126 models; the W220 had to do better.

SECs and CLs: The 140 Coupés

Just as with the previous W126 models, Stuttgart had always planned to offer expensive two-door coupé derivatives of the 140 range. These were ready in time to be announced at the Detroit Motor Show in January 1992, just a few months after the saloons had gone on sale. Showroom sales were scheduled to begin over the summer and autumn of 1992.

The new models did not meet with critical approval: in the UK, *Car* magazine memorably described the 600SEC on the show stand as 'ugly, thirsty and arrogant'. In view of the constraints imposed by their size, however, it must be said that Bruno Sacco's team had once again done an impressive job with the styling. The C140s seemed to blend elements of the W140 saloons with the superbly attractive lines of the W124 mid-range coupés that had been introduced in 1987 and were still in production. In those areas, they were a visual success. Much less successful, though, was the attempt to graft an SL-like nose on to the cars. Scaled up to fit, and blessed with curious wrapover headlamp units, it simply did not work.

Like the W126 coupés they replaced, the C140s sat on a short-wheelbase version of the saloon floor pan and shared its mechanical elements. Their wheelbase was 45mm (just under 2in) shorter than that of the standard-wheelbase W140 saloon. As befitted models with such pretensions, they were available

From this angle, the 140 coupé exuded an aura of power and wealth, which was exactly what many of those who bought the cars new were looking for. The car pictured is a 1991 model, and would have carried the original SEC badges.

A UK-registered S500 coupé dating from the 1995 model-year (pictures kindly supplied by Pete Lewis at Cheshire Classic Benz).

with only two engines, though, the flagship V12 600SEC being partnered by a V8 500SEC. It was perhaps fortunate that only big engines were specified, as, despite their smaller size, the new coupés weighed between 60kg and 80kg (130–175lb) more than the equivalent saloons.

The SECs of course shared much of their equipment and general specification with the saloons, including such features as the double-glazing. To this they added the electric seat-belt arm, which had been pioneered on the W126 coupés and was also on the contemporary W124 two-door models, power-operated rear head restraints and a self-dimming rear view mirror. A sports steering wheel was also standard equipment. Stuttgart had taken special care over the design of the front seats,

LEFT: *The interior of the 1995 S500 coupé illustrated on page 67.*

BELOW: *The styling of the C140 coupés reflected the spirit of the times, but has remained controversial. The cars always looked heavy, and lacked the delicacy of touch that had characterized their W126 coupé predecessors.*

which of course had to tip forward to provide access to the rear compartment, and these seats had a more cossetting shape than their broad, flat equivalents in the saloons.

From August 1993, the two coupés were renamed the S500 coupé and S600 coupé respectively, although the word 'coupé' never figured on the external badging. Confusingly, they were renamed yet again in June 1996, when they became the CL500 and CL600.

In the mean time, though, there had been some changes. April 1994 brought a new style of five-hole 18in alloy wheels in place of the eight-hole type on the earlier cars. Self-levelling rear suspension became standard on the S600 coupé while the heated front seat option became part of the standard S500 coupé package. Two years later, a new entry-level model was introduced with the 218bhp 4.2-litre V8 engine from the S420. The very first examples of this model, which arrived in April 1996, would in theory have worn S420 badges and been known as S420 coupés, but

After a period in which their designation changed not once, but twice, the C140 models emerged with the designation of CL class.

most countries only ever saw examples with the CL420 badge, which was introduced for the cars in June 1996.

With the new CL class designation in June 1996 came two additional changes: Parktronic parking radar front and rear was standardized

The wrapover front lamp units on the coupés were as much a statement of modernity as anything else. They certainly polarized opinions: people usually either loved them or hated them.

The 140 coupé looked much better in some colours than in others. This is a US-market car from 1998, finished in a rather attractive metallic gold.

along with nappa leather upholstery. From January 1997, Brake Assist became part of the standard specification, but there were no changes of note after that. The big coupés had found their own customer base and there was no point in Stuttgart putting a great

deal of effort into additional marketing and new models. There were still enough people prepared to pay outrageously high prices (top models were well over £100,000 in the UK) for what was, frankly, an outrageous car. Within a couple of years their production would in any case come to an end, and their replacements, the C215 coupés, promised a new start.

Special 140s

Although the W140s and C140s might have been out of tune with the prevailing economic conditions of their times, there are always some buyers who are blissfully unaffected by the economic problems of the rest of the world. Such buyers kept AMG and other tuners busy with requests for high-performance W140s during the 1990s. Not many of these buyers came from the UK, although in continental Europe such models as the 509bhp, 295km/h (185mph) 600SEL 6.9 from Brabus did find their mark.

When the W140 first reached the showrooms, Stuttgart's relationship with AMG had still not fully blossomed, and the AMG derivatives of the W140 were still seen as aftermarket confections. However, it was

<hr>

Best Buys

Various factors can influence purchase costs from time to time, and it is not possible to take these into account here. However, in terms of practicality and enjoyment, the following are the best W140 S class models to buy.

There is plenty of room for the average user and his or her family in a standard-wheelbase W140 saloon, so there is certainly no point in paying extra for a long-wheelbase model. The best engine choices are the S320 and S420, the former a six-cylinder and the latter a V8. The V12 is probably a little too exotic (and expensive) for most owners, while the S280 is a little pedestrian, and the diesels (not available in the UK) are even more so.

As for coupé models, there is no denying the allure of the S500's V8 power or of the V12's silken punch, but once again the 4.2-litre V8 model is probably the best choice to go for.

no surprise that the Affalterbach company quickly came up with its own enlarged V12 engine to produce the S73 model. With the 525bhp 7.3-litre engine that was also available in the SL roadsters (see Chapter 2), this monstrous power unit could be fitted to either saloon or coupé to produce an indecently quick machine. There were several other AMG options available to those who made a point of asking.

Stuttgart's increasing closeness to AMG was made vividly apparent in 1997 when the tuning company turned out to have been responsible for constructing a one-off S500 presented to Pope John Paul II in March that year. Strikingly good-looking without a fixed roof, this state landaulet made clear where some of the visual heaviness of the production design lay. The car followed in a tradition stretching back to 1930 of papal limousines being provided by Stuttgart. This time, however, the company was clearly looking upon AMG as its bespoke arm.

There were very rare body conversions available to well-heeled lesser mortals, too. Binz, a coachbuilder traditionally favoured by Mercedes, offered a beautifully proportioned Kombi (estate) version of the W140, which looked good enough to have been the factory's own work. The same coachbuilder also made at least one rather ungainly-looking high-roof ambulance for a European customer on the basis of the 177bhp S300 Turbodiesel.

Specifications for W140 Models

Engines

Petrol saloons

S280	2799cc M104 6-cyl, 193PS & 270Nm	(1993–1998)
300SE 2.8	2799cc M104 6-cyl, 193PS & 270Nm	(1993)
300SE	3199cc M104 6-cyl, 231PS & 310Nm	(1991–1993)
300SEL	3199cc M104 6-cyl, 231PS & 310Nm	(1991–1993)
S320	3199cc M104 6-cyl, 231PS & 315Nm	(1993–1998)
S320 (LWB)	3199cc M104 6-cyl, 231PS & 315Nm	(1993–1998)
400SE	4196cc M119 V8, 286PS & 410Nm	(1991–1992)
	4196cc M119 V8, 279PS & 400Nm	(1992–1993)
400SEL	4196cc M119 V8, 286PS & 410Nm	(1991–1992)
	4196cc M119 V8, 279PS & 400Nm	(1992–1993)
S420	4196cc M119 V8, 279PS & 400Nm	(1993–1998)
S420 (LWB)	4196cc M119 V8, 279PS & 400Nm	(1993–1998)
500SE	4973cc M119 V8, 326PS & 480Nm	(1991–1992)
	4973cc M119 V8, 320PS & 470Nm	(1992–1993)
500SEL	4973cc M119 V8, 326PS & 480Nm	(1991–1992)
	4973cc M119 V8, 320PS & 470Nm	(1992–1993)
S500	4973cc M119 V8, 320PS & 470Nm	(1993–1998)
S500 (LWB)	4973cc M119 V8, 320PS & 470Nm	(1993–1998)
600SE	5987cc M120 V12, 408PS & 580Nm	(1991–1992)
	5987cc M120 V12, 394PS & 570Nm	(1992–1993)
600SEL	5987cc M120 V12, 408PS & 580Nm	(1991–1992)
	5987cc M120 V12, 394PS & 570Nm	(1992–1993)
S600	5987cc M120 V12, 394PS & 570Nm	(1993–1998)
S600 (LWB)	5987cc M120 V12, 394PS & 570Nm	(1993–1998)

continued overleaf

Specifications for W140 Models *continued*

Engines *continued*

Diesel saloons

300SD	3449cc OM603 6-cyl, 150PS & 310Nm	(1991–1993)
S300 Turbodiesel	2996cc OM606 6-cyl, 177PS & 330Nm	(1996–1998)
S350 Turbodiesel	3449cc OM603 6-cyl, 150PS & 310Nm	(1993–1996)

Coupés

S420 Coupé	4196cc M119 V8, 279PS & 400Nm	(1994–1996)
CL420	4196cc M119 V8, 279PS & 400Nm	(1996–1998)
500SEC	4973cc M119 V8, 320PS & 470Nm	(1992–1993)
S500 Coupé	4973cc M119 V8, 320PS & 470Nm	(1993–1996)
CL500	4973cc M119 V8, 320PS & 470Nm	(1996–1998)
600SEC	5987cc M120 V12, 394PS & 570Nm	(1992–1993)
S600 Coupé	5987cc M120 V12, 394PS & 570Nm	(1993–1996)
CL600	5987cc M120 V12, 394PS & 570Nm	(1996–1998)

Transmissions

Five-speed manual (six-cylinder models only)
Four-speed automatic (to 1995)
Five-speed automatic (from 1995)

Running gear

Front suspension with twin wishbones, coil springs, gas dampers and anti-roll bar.
Rear suspension with five links, coil springs, gas dampers and anti-roll bar. Self-levelling optional on all six-cylinder and V8 models; ADS adaptive damping optional with self-levelling rear suspension; hydro-pneumatic suspension optional on V8 models and standard on V12 models.
Power-assisted recirculating-ball 'parameter' steering with variable ratio.
Four-wheel disc brakes, ventilated at the front only on 300SE and 300SEL and ventilated all round on other models: standard ABS, with servo assistance.
Tyres 225/60R16 (300SE and SEL) or 235/60ZR16 (V8 and V12 models).

Dimensions

Overall length:	5054mm (199in) (SEC &CL), 5113mm (201in) (SE) or 5213mm (205in) (SEL)
Wheelbase:	2945mm (116in) (coupés), 3040mm (120in) (SE) or 3140mm (124in) (SEL)
Overall width:	1886mm (74in) (saloons), 1905mm (75in) (coupés)
Overall height:	1455mm (57in) (coupés), 1495mm (59in) (saloons with hydro-pneumatic suspension), 1497mm (59in) (standard saloons)
Track:	1602mm (63in) (front); 1574mm (62in) (rear)

Weights (typical)

300SE:	1890kg (4158lb)
400SE:	1990kg (4378lb)
500SE:	2000kg (4400lb)
600SE:	2180kg (4796lb)
CL420 & CL500:	2080kg (4576lb)
CL600:	2240kg (4928lb)

Long-wheelbase models 100kg (220lb) heavier than standard saloons.

5　The Crucial C Class

W202 Models, 1993–2001

When Mercedes engineers and designers started work on the second-generation compact Mercedes, in September 1986, they had a tough act to follow. The W201 or '190' range, introduced four years earlier, in 1982, had been Stuttgart's attempt to wrest leadership of its market sector away from the BMW 3 Series, and it had certainly given Mercedes' arch-rival a run for its money. The battle was still raging, and would do so for several more years before the new compact Mercedes made it into production, but Stuttgart's engineers already had a

clear idea of the changes they would need to make for the new model, which would be coded W202.

The most significant of the W201's shortcomings was a lack of rear legroom, so the next-generation car would have to do better in that area. (In fact, this would be addressed to some extent at the car's 1988 mid-life facelift.) Also important would be a wider range of engines than the W201s had offered, and the new car had to appeal to a younger audience, too: while Mercedes had hoped that the W201 would appeal to the same younger buyers who enjoyed the 3 Series models, in practice they

This early W202 belonged to the Mercedes-Benz UK press fleet, and was pictured on the road course at the Millbrook proving ground. The car was solidly built, but driving it was quite a forgettable experience!

had found that the majority of buyers were older individuals who were downsizing!

These requirements had to be incorporated into an ambitious overall design package for the new W202s, which were being drawn up as the basis of a whole gamut of forthcoming Mercedes model ranges. Not only would there be saloons as direct replacements for the W201s, but there would also be estate variants, to compete with the BMW 3 Series estates. On top of that, the basic 'platform' of the new compact saloon would also be used for spin-off models: a two-door coupé and cabriolet (which later materialized as the W208 CLKs), and an 'affordable' roadster (which became the R170 SLK).

Two items seen on rival manufacturers' cars were quickly ruled out as work progressed.

Four-wheel-drive, seen on some BMW 3 Series variants, was seen as too heavy and too expensive, while its potential market (mainly in the Alpine regions of Europe) was too small to justify the development time and costs. Four-wheel steering, seen on some Honda models, was considered unnecessary on a car of the W202's size.

The initial styling ideas were turned into five full-size clay models during 1987. Within a year, the essential specification of the W202 had been settled. Styling details were finalized and testing began on major new components, such as the double-wishbone suspension that the engineers had drawn up. The first machine tools were in place by June 1990, and more than fifty representative prototypes of the new car were made and tested. Anticipated build

Handling was thoroughly competent right from the start, but the cars never conveyed the same sharpness and sense of involvement that were present in even the humblest of their competitors from BMW.

volumes were high enough for Stuttgart to arrange assembly in two plants – Bremen and Sindelfingen – where production proper began at the end of 1992, for a 1993 sales launch.

By this stage, too, the important decision had been taken to give the new compact saloon a new name for public consumption. It would not be the 'new 190' but instead it would be called the C class, that letter reflecting its 'compact' size.

Design

Although it would still be 'compact' by the standards of contemporary Mercedes cars, the new C class was drawn up as a bigger car than its predecessor. Its wheelbase was an inch longer to allow for a longer passenger cabin and better ride, while its nose was 50mm (2in) longer to give better crash performance. Yet careful packaging, which included siting the 62-litre fuel tank under the rear seat, allowed the car to be no more than 39mm (1.5in) longer overall than the W201.

It was inevitably somewhat heavier, though. The extra length added a few kilos, while thicker sheet metal in some areas and tough side-impact beams in the doors did the rest. Weighing between 16 and 18 per cent more than their predecessors on a model-for-model basis, the W202s were never going to be overtly sporting cars, and in due course would attract unfavourable comparison with their BMW rivals for that very reason.

Whereas the W201s had been fashionably slab-sided in the 1980s mould, the W202s anticipated the softer shapes of the 1990s, with more rounded contours. A steeper bonnet rake, changes in the rear roof line and the angle of the rear screen, and flush side glazing all made for a more aerodynamic shape. On the W201s, the Cd average had been 0.33; for the W202s, it varied between 0.30 and 0.32.

The 'chassis' meanwhile had also been improved, and the W202s benefited from a very comfortable and quiet ride, allied to very

Mercedes' aim was to give the interiors a fresh look that would appeal to younger buyers, but in the beginning they came up with some howlers, such as this trim pattern and colour.

secure handling, marred only by a rather wooden steering feel from the power-assisted recirculating-ball system. The superb five-link rear suspension that the W201s had pioneered was changed only in minor details, but the front suspension was completely altered. The old cars' McPherson struts gave way to a new double-wishbone layout, similar to that also being prepared for the W140 S class (*see* Chapter 4) but made of pressed steel rather than aluminium and without the anti-dive properties of the S class.

The thinking behind this was that it would improve ride refinement and handling: the W201s' struts had been subject to bending loads, which increased damper friction. The short upper wishbone – in fact, a single lateral link rather than a triangulated 'A' arm – allowed for a wide engine bay, while hollow bushes containing hydraulic damping fluid

Matching the colour of the fascia to that of the seats really did not help when the basic colour was so lurid!

Development, Dieter Zetsche), and reflected the company's new philosophy that the customer, rather than the engineers, knew best. It was also undeniable that the interior mouldings seemed more flimsy than those on earlier Mercedes, and this was no doubt a result of an early 1990s directive to cut production costs.

The driving position, though, was better than in the W201, with more seat-height adjustment. The dash design was similar to that which would appear first in the W140 S class, with a smaller instrument cluster and a lower cowl than before, plus back-lit instruments. Unlike the W201s, however, the W202s were designed with a US-style foot-operated parking brake, while a drawback on RHD cars was that the steering column was offset from the centre line. As for the rear seat, it was designed with a split-folding backrest (although this would not be available on all models) and an access panel to the boot, which together allowed longer loads to be carried. The car also had 50mm (2in) more legroom than the earlier compact saloons.

Safety features abounded, of course, and when the cars were launched Mercedes described them all as being governed by a philosophy known as ICASIS (Integrated Car Impact Safety System). As well as the door impact beams, the relocated fuel tank and ABS, there were also pyrotechnic safety-belt tensioners, while a driver's airbag was made standard and a passenger's side bag optional. Mercedes publicity emphasized the fact that all airbags were the full-size variety rather than the smaller ones permitted in Europe; in fact, it must have simplified production to use the full-size bags on all models when they were obligatory on cars destined for the US anyway.

Publicity also stressed that the car had been conceived with recycling in mind – something which could only have happened in Germany with its strong Green political lobby! The W202s were designed to make end-of-life dismantling quick and easy (it was no longer politically correct to speak of 'scrapping'), and around 12 per cent of each car was actually

were fitted at the rear inboard pivot of the wishbone to give good control and low noise transmission. Similar bushes supported the differential on the rear sub-frame, for the same reasons.

By this stage, it was only to be expected that ABS would be a standard feature on the new car; a three-channel system was chosen. There were already plans for various traction control systems that would piggy-back on this. Brakes were of course going to be discs all round once again.

All this was traditional engineering-led thinking from Mercedes-Benz, but the interior hinted at the company's new approach. Controversially, there was no oil-pressure gauge (a Mercedes tradition for over 40 years); instead, there was a conventional warning light. The decision to make this change had been made only a year before the new model's launch (by the new Director of Product

made of recycled materials. This particularly affected the plastic components, and every one that weighed 100 grammes or more was marked with a material identification code to simplify onward recycling. The number of different plastics used was also minimized for the same reason.

1993: The C180, C220, C220 Diesel and C 250 Diesel

Stuttgart was already planning for a very wide model range in the 202 series, but had wisely decided not to put all the new models on to the market at once. Saloons would come first, to be followed by estates within three years, and only the lower-ranking models of the saloon range would appear in the beginning. This would ensure that there was a ready demand when the high-performance and more expensive top models became available later.

The W202s that went on sale in the autumn of 1993 consisted of two petrol four-cylinders (the C180 and C220) and two diesels (the four-cylinder C220 Diesel and the five-cylinder C250 Diesel). Lowest-powered was the C220 Diesel, with 95bhp. Next up was the 115bhp C250 Diesel, followed by the 122bhp C180 and the 150bhp C220. The 2.2-litre petrol engine was a 16-valve type, which had proved itself in the later W124 models, while the 1.8-litre engine was a derivative of it, and was seen for the first time in the W202s. Both the diesels were newly revised versions of earlier engines, featuring four valves per cylinder – a world first for diesel engines. Both also had oxidation catalysts and an electronically controlled EGR (Exhaust Gas Recirculation) system, to reduce harmful emissions.

Of these initial W202s, the 'performance' model was the C220, which delivered a respectable 205km/h (129mph) and could reach 100km/h from rest in 10.5 seconds. The other models were fairly pedestrian, though: the C220 Diesel needed 17.4 seconds to hit 100km/h and peaked at 171km/h (107mph), the C250 Diesel needed 15.6 seconds to reach

Smoked glass for the rear light lenses arrived on the later cars.

the benchmark speed and ran out of steam at 185km/h (116mph), and the C180 took 13 seconds to reach 60mph and could not exceed 189km/h (118mph). This lack of performance was the main reason why the C180 had a front anti-roll bar only while all the other models had one at the rear as well. Refinement was good in the diesel models, thanks to the engine encapsulation, which had so effectively minimized compression-ignition 'knock' on more recent Mercedes models. It was good in the C180, too, although the C220 seemed strangely harsh, a surprise after the engine had sounded so refined in its W124 application.

As always, both manual and automatic transmissions were on offer. The manual, a five-speed, was quite widely criticized for its wide gear spacing and baulky gearchange with long shift travel. The clutch, too, had a disappointingly long travel. The four-speed automatic was a very much better option, and came with switchable Economy and Sport modes. In many countries, it proved the popular choice.

Calling the new car a C class (the C standing for 'compact') was part of the new Mercedes-Benz model nomenclature, but another first for the company was a series of four specification levels for each new model. These had been carefully prepared to appeal to each of the four key customer types that the company expected for the W202s, and a badge just behind each front wheel revealed the specification level of each car.

The Classic trim level was aimed at the traditional Mercedes buyer, and brought standard suspension settings with deliberately sober and low-key interior appointments. By contrast, the Esprit trim was aimed at younger buyers, and delivered suspension lowered by 20mm (just under an inch), with much brighter interior trim. There were grey plastic trim strips on the bumpers, the door trims and console, and

The styling was unmistakably Mercedes, but somehow it always looked just a little bland. This is an early UK press picture, showing the Elegance trim level.

Alloy wheels undoubtedly did a lot for the car's appearance. This is an early C200.

on the dash top. This trim level also brought a split-folding rear seat with its own armrest.

Elegance was the luxury trim level, with standard suspension settings but bright metal trim and wood inserts on the dash, console and doors, allied to a range of sober colours. An electric glass sunroof, electric windows, front and rear armrests, and leather trim on the steering wheel and gear knob were all part of the package. While cloth was the standard upholstery material on this as well as the other trim levels, the Elegance trim probably went best with extra-cost leather upholstery.

The fourth specification level was Sport, which meant suspension lowered by 23mm (almost an inch) from standard, firmer dampers, bigger anti-roll bars, 205/60 tyres, machined aluminium trim strips on the B-pillars outside and on the console, doors and dashboard inside, a smaller sports steering wheel and sports seats with additional lateral support, plus, of course, a leather option. In addition, the steering ratio was quicker, at 3.2:1 instead of the standard 3.4:1.

1994: The C200, C200 Diesel and C280

In theory, the W202 range was launched with a total of seven engine options, and those who attended the press launch in 1993 were able to drive examples of each. In practice, however, three engines did not become available until the early months of 1994. These were the range-topping six-cylinder in the C280, the mid-range 2-litre petrol engine in the C200, and the entry-level diesel in the C200 Diesel.

The C280 of course took over from the 190E 2.6, which had enjoyed mixed fortunes as the top-of-the-range W201 model. With the Elegance trim it appealed to the buyers who had warmed to the older car, while with the Sport specification it delivered what more sporting drivers had sought but never found in the six-cylinder W201. The straight-six engine was the same M104 four-valver, which had proved itself so well in the final W124 medium-sized cars, and gave both high levels of refinement and plenty of performance if

At the top of the 'everyday' petrol range was always a 2.8-litre engine. Initially it was the old M104 straight-six, but from 1997 the M112 V6 (seen here) took over.

pushed hard. With 193bhp it propelled the C280 to a top speed of 225km/h (141mph), polished off the 0–100km/h sprint in 8.5 seconds and offered excellent high-speed acceleration.

The C200's engine was quite a lot less exciting, but it plugged a gap in the range between the C180 and C220 models. Like the C280's straight-six, this four-valve four-cylinder had been seen in the final W124 models, and was a well-proven powerplant. With 136bhp, it endowed the W202 with a 197km/h (123mph) maximum and 0–60mph acceleration of 11.4 seconds – respectable, but designed to appeal more to those who were likely to specify the Classic, Elegance or Esprit trim levels than to those who wanted the Sport version.

Last came the bargain-basement C200 Diesel, which was the only one of the early W202s not to use the latest four-valve engine technology. Instead, it had the old two-valve 2-litre diesel engine, and with just 75bhp it was something of a plodder although it was reasonably economical. Like the C180, this model was slow enough not to need a rear anti-roll

bar, and it was not made available in all Mercedes' markets. The UK, in particular, managed without it.

1994: The C36 AMG

Striking though that C280 was, especially when allied to the Sport specification, the next W202 release made it clear that Mercedes aimed to take on the high-performance models of the BMW 3 Series as well. June 1994 brought an eighth engine to the W202 range in the shape of an AMG-developed M104 six-cylinder that had been bored and stroked to give a swept volume of 3.6 litres. It went into a car called the C36 AMG, small brother of the existing E36 AMG.

Of course, the C36 AMG was always intended as a small-volume niche model, and just 5200 examples would be built in three seasons of production. Stuttgart never really expected it to sell in the same volumes as BMW's well-established M3, which was its most obvious rival. One factor inhibiting higher sales volumes must have been its showroom price – in the UK, it cost half as much again as a C280 – but the Mercedes people were content to let the C36 find its own small but discerning group of customers.

Their money bought them a comfortable but compact four-door saloon, with all the expected Mercedes refinements and a 0–60mph acceleration time of under 7 seconds. There was colossal torque all the way through the rev range, giving effortless acceleration, while the twin-pipe exhaust (with an AMG logo cast into each outlet) emitted a sporting bark when the car was pressed hard. Roadholding and handling on the wider tyres (225/45ZR17s on the front and 245/40ZR17s on the rear) were superb, while AMG's quicker steering box made the car feel like a proper sporting machine. Maximum speed was limited to 250km/h (155mph) under the usual German 'gentlemen's agreement' among manufacturers, but there is no doubt that the C36's 280bhp would have taken it on to far higher speeds without the restrictor built into its engine-management system. Astonishingly, 25mpg (11.3ltr/100km) was a realistic possibility, although a C36 AMG was more likely to return around 20mpg (14ltr/100km) in town driving.

Every C36 AMG started life as a Sport-trimmed car with automatic transmission on Mercedes' own assembly lines alongside lesser C classes, but it was then shipped in a partially finished state to AMG's works. Here, the suspension was lowered and stiffened, the steering was tweaked, the special engine was fitted, and the special 17in wheels and body kit were added. Inside, a 270km/h (170mph) speedometer was fitted, along with a special gear knob with 'C36' impressed into the leather. Leather upholstery was still an extra-cost option, but AMG would also produce special interior trim and colours to order.

1995–1996: The Estates, the C230, C230 Kompressor and C250 Turbodiesel

There had been an early perception that the W202 was a rather conservative car, certainly lacking in the sporting appeal of the rival BMW 3 Series. This may be what lay behind a number of upgrades that were announced in September 1995. Wider front tracks and 195/65R15 tyres in place of the early models' 185/65s suggested that Stuttgart was focusing

Alloy wheels were part of the Esprit specification for the UK right from the start.

on handling improvements as a way of improving sales. But much more important as a way of drawing attention to the range was the arrival of a C230 Kompressor model.

The C230 Kompressor was the first model from Stuttgart to use the new supercharged version of the 2.3-litre M111 four-cylinder engine, although others would follow soon.

With 193bhp and a good strong spread of torque, it gave the affordable four-cylinder model a much more sporting feel – although, sadly, the exhaust note was always disappointingly flat.

However, major range expansion had to wait until May 1996, and it came with the introduction of what Stuttgart always knew as

The most important model in the middle of the W202 range was the C230 Kompressor, powered by the 2.3-litre supercharged four-cylinder engine seen here.

The 2.5-litre turbocharged five-cylinder engine provided the C250 Turbodiesel models with strong lugging power, but it was an old-school engine with indirect injection and was completely eclipsed by the later common-rail diesels.

The estate models were better-looking than the saloons. Their compact dimensions ensured that they would never have the interior volume of the larger E class cars, although they were useful family load-haulers. This 1996 UK car has the Sport specification.

the T-Model, familiarly known in English-speaking countries as the 'estate'. This was a new departure for the C class, as there had never been an estate variant of the W201 range that had preceded the W202s. However, the success of estate variants of the rival BMW 3 Series cars had probably been the catalyst in the development of this range extension.

Like the BMWs, the estate versions of the W202 (strictly known as S202 types) were more lifestyle accessories than load-luggers. Load space was limited to 1510litres (53cu ft) with the rear seats folded, and to a mere 465 litres (16cu ft) with all seats in use. Nevertheless, the time was obviously right, as the estates found a ready market. They came with the same four equipment levels as the saloons – Classic, Elegance, Esprit and Sport – and a choice of six engines. These were three diesels (C200 Diesel, C220 Diesel and C250 Turbodiesel, although the 2.2-litre model was only for Portugal) and three petrol types

(C180, C200 and C230). The 2.3-litre naturally aspirated engine was new to both the estates and the saloons, and was of course simply the supercharged 2.3-litre engine without its supercharger. In the UK, however, it did not prove popular and was withdrawn after a year. All these estates were built at the Mercedes-Benz plant in Bremen, alongside the W202 saloons.

Some rarer models followed. August 1996 brought a C220 Diesel for the taxi market, with an engine prepared for bio-diesel that was considerably down on power, and a C200 Kompressor estate for Italy, Greece and Portugal followed in September 1996. Meanwhile, the whole 202 range benefited in August 1996 from the introduction of five-speed automatic gearboxes to replace the four-speed types. These had Summer and Winter settings, the latter obviously giving more measured acceleration to suit poorer road conditions.

The arrival of the CDI diesel engines gave the 202 range a much-needed boost. This is an estate model C220 CDI.

1997: V6 Engines, Facelift and C43 AMG

The pace of improvement did not let up and in June 1997 Stuttgart gave the 202 range its mid-life facelift and introduced a number of new variants.

The facelifted cars were easy enough to recognize. They had redesigned front and rear aprons with a more pronounced tuck-under, plus side sills painted in the body colour. The tail lights took on smoked indicator lenses, and there was a new selection of alloy wheel styles. Interior trim and some of the switchgear were also changed.

All of this concealed technological changes under the skin. The most significant were two new engines, of which more in a moment, but the 202 range would from now on be more dependent on electronic aids. Sadly, early models often suffered from problems with this

new equipment because build quality could be a little patchy. There was a new ASSYST Active Service System, which monitored the condition of the engine oil and advised when a service was due. Electronic Brake Assist detected the onset of an emergency stop and automatically applied maximum braking power, and the ELCODE key provided keyless locking and greater security against theft.

The new engines were the very latest three-valve all-aluminium V6s of the M112 family. A 2.4-litre type replaced the 2.3-litre four-cylinder engine, so raising the stakes in that area of the market by providing both greater refinement and extra prestige. This created the C240, available as both saloon and estate. Above this was a 2.8-litre engine, which replaced the now elderly M104 straight-six in the C280 models and took on the old designation. Here, however, it was perhaps less successful than its smaller sibling. The old 2.8-litre

RIGHT, TOP: For real excitement from a W202, you had to aim for the C43 AMG model with its tuned V8 engine. This was the under-bonnet view.

RIGHT, CENTRE: Instead of the Mercedes star, the AMG model carried this badge on its nose.

RIGHT, BOTTOM: AMG always offered their own design of alloy wheels, as seen on this C43 model.

six had been a notably smooth engine, and some early examples of the 2.8-litre V6 were noticeably rougher.

Also introduced in June 1997 was a replacement for the C36 AMG, of which production had ended earlier that year. Once again completed by AMG from a partially finished Sport variant, the C43 AMG brought V8 power to the W202 range for the first time.

It was, of course, an expensive low-production model. The heart of the new car was AMG's version of the 4.3-litre Mercedes V8 seen in the company's larger saloon ranges. Power was 306bhp at 5850rpm, but this was academic in a car that was once again limited electronically to 250km/h (155mph). More important was the huge torque of 297lb ft, developed all the way from 3250rpm to 5000rpm, which delivered effortless acceleration at all reasonable speeds right up to the 6500rpm redline.

The secrets of the AMG V8 were hotter camshafts, a switchable intake plenum, larger-diameter intake tracts and a special exhaust system. This had a free-flow manifold to reduce

As always, the AMG model was quite discreet. However, there was no mistaking what this car was, with twin exhaust outlets and the AMG badge on the boot lid.

How Fast? How Thirsty?

These figures are typical for W202 C class saloons, but variations in the car's equipment levels and load, and variations in driving style will cause differences that may be significant. Estate variants can be slightly slower and thirstier.

	0–60mph	Max speed	Mpg (overall)
C200 Diesel	19.6sec (manual)	158km/h (99mph)	37 (7.6ltr/100km)
C220 Diesel	16.3sec (manual)	174km/h (109mph)	33 (8.5ltr/100km)
C220 CDI	10.5sec (manual)	197km/h (123mph)	46 (6.15ltr/100km)
C250 Diesel	15.3sec (auto)	187km/h (116mph)	33 (8.4ltr/100km)
C180	12.0sec (manual)	192km/h (120mph)	26 (10.8ltr/100km)
C200 Kompressor	8.8sec (manual, to Aug 1996)	225km/h (140mph)	23 (12.3ltr/100km)
C230	10.5sec (manual)	208km/h (130mph)	26 (10.8ltr/100km)
C230 Kompressor	8.4sec (manual)	230km/h (143mph)	27 (10.5ltr/100km)
C240	9.9sec (auto)	213km/h (133mph)	24 (11.8ltr/100km)
C280 (V6)	8.5sec (auto)	227km/h (142mph)	25 (11.3ltr/100km)
C36 AMG	6.7sec	250km/h (155mph) (limited)	20 (14ltr/100km)
C43 AMG	6.5sec	250km/h (155mph) (limited)	21.5 (13ltr/100km)
C55 AMG	5.5sec	250km/h (155mph) (limited)	22.5 (12.5ltr/100km)

Various factors can influence purchase costs from time to time, and it is not possible to take these into account here. However, in terms of practicality and enjoyment, these are the best W202 C class models to buy.

The choice of saloon or estate is purely down to individual taste, but it is worth remembering that the C202 estates have a modest load capacity and are not huge load-luggers in the style of the mid-range (E class) Mercedes. Variations in trim level are also down to individual preferences, but in most countries the cheaper and smaller-engined cars usually came with cloth trim while leather was only common in more expensive models such as the six-cylinders.

If running costs are no object, then one of the AMG models is a must-have. The six-cylinder C36 was always an exciting machine and remains so, even though the later V8-powered models are quicker. But

for most people, one of the more mundane saloons will prove a best buy.

As always with Mercedes-Benz, the six-cylinder engines have much more character than the four-cylinders. The V6 types are not as much of an improvement over the older straight-sixes as Mercedes would have liked buyers to believe, although there is certainly nothing else to their detriment.

The Kompressor models are undoubtedly the best of the four-cylinder petrol W202s and deliver a satisfying punch, although they do have a disappointingly flat and uninspiring exhaust note. However, the real stars of the range are the later CDI diesel engines, which combine excellent fuel economy (and, therefore, running costs) with really strong performance. A C220 CDI may not out-accelerate lesser cars away from the traffic lights, but in every other respect it is an outstandingly good all-rounder for everyday use.

back-pressure and two large-volume silencers, while there were also twin ceramic catalytic converters. Always allied to the latest five-speed automatic gearbox with an adaptive shift programme and the Summer and Winter modes, this engine put its power on the road through the same 17in wheels and wide tyres as the car it replaced. Twin chrome tailpipes, a body kit of sills and front and rear aprons, and AMG's characteristic monoblock wheels all added visual distinction without making the car too ostentatious.

However, there was ostentation for the asking on the inside, where optional two-tone leather allowed customers to indulge in some questionable taste. Designo LCP paint on the outside could also be ordered, although its ability to change colour with the light and the viewing angle was more gimmicky than ostentatious. And this time around, the AMG car could be had not only as a saloon but also as an estate. Needless to say, ESP stability control, Speedtronic cruise control, the ASSYST Service Interval Indicator and Brake Assist were all included in the package.

1998–1999: Common-Rail Diesels and the C55 AMG

It would be hard to over-estimate the impact that the arrival of Mercedes' new common-rail diesel engines had on the diesel-car scene. Common-rail injection, in which the fuel is injected directly into the cylinders under very high pressure, was already known on diesel engines for commercial vehicles, but the new Mercedes CDI diesels were the first to bring it to a production car. They combined the new technology with turbochargers and intercoolers.

A single example makes clear how common-rail injection transformed the diesel passenger-car engine: in May 1998, the C220 CDI with its new OM611 engine and a swept volume of 2151cc replaced the C220 Diesel with its 2155cc OM604 engine. The new engine delivered 300Nm of torque at lower engine speeds than those needed by the old one to deliver just half as much. It was a revelation.

For Stuttgart, the advent of common-rail engines would also lead to savings in production costs. The common-rail engines were much more readily 'tunable' than the older direct-injection and indirect-injection engines, and it became possible to offer the same engine in different states of tune for different models. So the C200 CDI that joined the range had the same 2151cc engine as the C220 CDI, but with different programming of its electronic control system, so that it delivered just 102PS instead of 125PS.

These, though, were to be the only CDI engines that would be used in the 202 range. The five-cylinder OM612 and six-cylinder OM613 common-rail diesels would be confined to larger and more expensive Mercedes models.

The advent of the CDI engines was not the only news as the 1998 model-year drew to a close. Announced in June was a new top model from AMG to replace the C43 AMG. This one was called the C55 AMG and boasted the Affalterbach company's latest 5.5-litre derivative of the M113 three-valve V8 engine.

Squeezing this big engine into the W202 had resulted in some minor compromises, and the engine delivered just 347PS instead of the 354PS seen in other AMG Mercedes. However, the same 510Nm of torque delivered astonishing performance – 0–60mph in 5.5 seconds in the saloon and 5.7 seconds in the estate – and an axle ratio taller than in the superseded C43 AMG gave easy high-speed cruising. Of course, the engine was speed-limited to 250km/h (155mph), but no doubt some aftermarket specialists were able to remove that little restriction...

The C55 AMG was built in tiny numbers to special order, with only forty-five examples of the saloon being constructed. Figures for the estate variant are not known, but they were almost certainly smaller.

2000–2001: The End

The last significant modification for the 202 range was the standardization of the ESP stability control system during the 1999

Later interiors were easier on the eye. This is the driver's environment on a 2001 model, actually one of the estates.

season. By that time, the range's days were numbered. Production of the saloons ended in September 2000, when they were replaced by the new W203 range models. The estates, however, remained in production until May 2001, when they in turn were replaced by W203 derivatives.

Those last few months demanded an interesting balancing act as estate customers held back from buying their cars in anticipation of the arrival of the new W203 versions. Around the world, Mercedes adopted a variety of strategies. In the UK they decided to boost customer interest by introducing the C200 Kompressor estate, a model that had not been available in that market before.

Epilogue

Even though the 202 range was being built at a time when Mercedes' quality control was at a low ebb, it did extremely well for Stuttgart. It overtook the E class to become the marque's best-seller for most of its production life, and in its best year of 1998 almost 320,000 examples were built.

Specifications for W202 Models

Engines

Petrol saloons

C180	1799cc M111 4-cyl, 122PS & 170Nm	(1993–2000)
C200	1998cc M111 4-cyl, 136PS & 190Nm	(1994–2000)
C200 Kompressor	1998cc M111 4-cyl, 184PS & 260Nm	(1995–1996)
	1998cc M111 4-cyl, 192PS & 270Nm	(1995–2000)
C220	2199cc M111 4-cyl, 150PS & 210Nm	(1993–1996)
C230	2295cc M111 4-cyl, 150PS & 220Nm	(1996–1997)
	2295cc M111 4-cyl, 150PS & 210Nm	(1997–1998)
C230 Kompressor	2295cc M111 4-cyl, 193PS & 280Nm	(1996–2000)
C240	2398cc M112 V6, 170PS & 225Nm	(1997–2000)
C280	2799cc M104 6-cyl, 193PS & 270Nm	(1993–1997)
	2799cc M112 V6, 197PS & 265Nm	(1997–2000)
C36 AMG	3606cc M104 6-cyl, 280PS & 385Nm	(1993–1997)
C43 AMG	4266cc M113 V8, 306PS & 410Nm	(1997–2000)
C55 AMG	5439cc M113 V8, 347PS & 510Nm	(1998–2000)

Diesel saloons

C200 Diesel	1997cc OM601 4-cyl, 75PS & 130Nm	(1993–1995)
	1997cc OM601 4-cyl, 88PS & 135Nm	(1996–1997)
	1997cc OM604 4-cyl, 88PS & 135Nm	(1997–1998)
C200 CDI	2151cc OM611 4-cyl, 102PS & 235Nm	(1998–1999)
	2148cc OM611 4-cyl, 102PS & 235Nm	(1999–2000)
C220 Diesel	2155cc OM604 4-cyl, 95PS & 150Nm	(1993–1998)
	2155cc OM604 4-cyl, 75PS & 150Nm (Bio-diesel version)	(1998–1999)
C220 CDI	2151cc OM611 4-cyl, 125PS & 300Nm	(1998–1999)
	2148cc OM611 4-cyl, 125PS & 300Nm	(1999–2000)
C250 Diesel	2497cc OM605 5-cyl, 113PS & 170Nm	(1993–1996)
C250 Turbodiesel	2497cc OM605 5-cyl, 150PS & 280Nm	(1995–2000)

continued overleaf

Specifications for W202 Models *continued*

Engines *continued*

Petrol estates

C180	1799cc M111 4-cyl, 122PS & 170Nm	(1996–2000)
	1998cc M111 4-cyl, 129PS & 190Nm	(2000–2001)
C200	1998cc M111 4-cyl, 136PS & 190Nm	(1997–2000)
C200 Kompressor	1998cc M111 4-cyl, 192PS & 270Nm	(1996–2000)
	1998cc M111 4-cyl, 163PS & 230Nm	(2000–2001)
C230	2295cc M111 4-cyl, 150PS & 210Nm	(1996–1998)
C230 Kompressor	2295cc M111 4-cyl, 193PS & 280Nm	(1997–2000)
C240	2398cc M112 V6, 170PS & 225Nm	(1997–2000)
	2398cc M112 V6, 170PS & 240Nm	(2000–2001)
C280	2799cc M112 V6, 197PS & 265Nm	(1997–2000)
C43 AMG	4266cc M113 V8, 306PS & 410Nm	(1997–2000)
C55 AMG	5439cc M113 V8, 347PS & 510Nm	(1998–2000)

Diesel estates

C200 Diesel	1997cc OM604 4-cyl, 88PS & 135Nm	(1996–1997)
C200 CDI	2151cc OM611 4-cyl, 102PS & 235Nm	(1998–1999)
	2148cc OM611 4-cyl, 102PS & 235Nm	(1999–2001)
C220 Diesel	2155cc OM604 4-cyl, 95PS & 150Nm	(1996–1997)
C220 CDI	2151cc OM611 4-cyl, 125PS & 300Nm	(1998–1999)
	2148cc OM611 4-cyl, 125PS & 300Nm	(1999–2001)
C250 Turbodiesel	2497cc OM605 5-cyl, 150PS & 280Nm	(1996–1997)

Transmissions

Five-speed manual or four-speed automatic up to mid-1996; thereafter five-speed manual or five-speed automatic. No manual option on AMG cars; some other models sold only with automatic transmissions in some countries.

Running gear

Front suspension with twin unequal-length wishbones, coil springs, gas dampers and anti-roll bar. Rear suspension with five links, coil springs, gas dampers and anti-roll bar (no rear anti-roll bar on C180 or C200 Diesel).
Power-assisted recirculating-ball steering with 3.4:1 ratio (3.2:1 ratio on Sport models).
Four-wheel disc brakes, ventilated at front on some models and at the rear on C43 AMG and C55 AMG; three-channel ABS standard, with servo assistance. Tyres 195/65VR15 (standard) or 205/60VR15 (Sport models); 225/45ZR17 front and 245/40ZR17 rear on all AMG models.

Dimensions

Overall length:	4487mm (177in)
Wheelbase:	2690mm (106in)
Overall width:	1720mm (68in)
Overall height:	1418mm (56in)
Track:	1499mm (59in) (front); later 1505mm (59in); 1464mm (58in) (rear)

Weights (typical)

C180:	1350kg (2970lb)
C200:	1365kg (3003lb)
C200D:	1400kg (3080lb)
C230:	1410kg (3102lb)
C230 Kompressor:	1420kg (3124lb)
C250 Turbodiesel:	1480kg (3256lb)
C280:	1490kg (3278lb)
C43 AMG:	1500kg (3300lb)

6 Mid-Range Master

The W210 Saloons and Estates

The mid-range Mercedes, known as the E class since 1992, had always been the company's biggest seller. The W124 range introduced in the mid-1980s had set the benchmark for its class and in 11 years of production actually sold more than any other Mercedes-Benz range built before or since – a massive 2.7 million examples. However, the brief for the W124 replacement was to be very different. For a start, there would be no coupé or cabriolet derivatives, as the plan was to build the replacements for these models on the C class platform. It was also quite clear that the new mid-range Mercedes would have a shorter production life than that of the range it replaced: buyers now expected more frequent changes of model and the new one would be designed to remain competitive for no more than eight years. Although there was never any chance, therefore, that the new W210 E class

This 2001-model W210 was one of a special edition for the USA. Note the US-specification side marker lights in the front bumper wraparounds.

would out-sell the W124s in terms of total sales, in fact the W210s sold more briskly than the range they replaced. By the time they had been in production for four years they had already sold a million examples, to become the market leader in their class. For Mercedes, this was a major success, and a vindication of its redesign of the mid-range cars.

Preliminary work for the W210 included an examination of the W124's shortcomings. The range was still selling strongly in the early 1990s, still widely respected and still considered the benchmark in the medium-size sector. But BMW had stolen a march on its rather austere styling with their attractive E34 5 Series models; the sportier handling of the BMWs also gave them an appeal that the W124s did not have. Clearly, both styling and handling had to be improved on the new Mercedes.

The twin oval light units, pioneered on a concept model of what became the CLK, gave the 210 a distinctive 'face' with just the right combination of tradition and modernity.

A major success for the W124 range had been the estates, and the BMW rival was nowhere near as capacious as the Mercedes. However, the W124s were under pressure from other rivals, notably Volvo, so it was clear that the new Mercedes estate would have to retain its load-carrying ability, or perhaps even improve on it.

Most important of all was the fact that the new W210 E class was to be wholly engineered under the new Mercedes policy of focusing on manufacturing cost and customer demand. The W202 C class had been partially engineered under this new regime, but the W210 was the real test of the new approach. In Mercedes' own terms, it proved a great success because the new E class cost 20 per cent less to build than the model it replaced. In customer terms, however, it was very much less successful: the cost savings were all too evident in a number of areas and many cars developed a rust problem unacceptably early in their lives.

Design

The dimensional package drawn up for the new W210 E class added 33mm (1.25in) to the wheelbase of the W124s, all of it in the rear cabin. An increase in width by 59mm (2.25in) allowed Mercedes later to boast that interior room matched that in the short-wheelbase W126 S class. The estate models, designed alongside the saloons, had a longer rear overhang to retain their load-carrying supremacy, and it is interesting to note that the saloons were originally designed with the same long rear end to give a huge boot. It was only late on in the design process that the overhang was shortened, apparently mainly on aesthetic grounds.

The suspension system was designed to give a combination of exceptional ride comfort and tight control, so the rear end had a modified version of the much-admired five-link system while the front had the double wishbones seen in the latest C class and S class

Sober, not very exciting, but dependable and prestigious: the E230 Classic saloon as offered to the British public in 1995.

instead of the separate damper and strut arrangement of the W124. Anti-roll bars were standard front and rear, and the optional Sport suspension, which replaced the earlier Sportline option, brought a lower ride height with springs and dampers that were 10 per cent stiffer than standard. As for the steering, a variable-ratio rack-and-pinion system gave much more feel and was both cheaper and lighter than the older type. With the Sport suspension came a quicker ratio.

Styling the saloon and estate models together ensured that the estate had an integrated appearance and did not look as if the rear end had been added to a saloon as an afterthought. The W210 was also the first production Mercedes to have the twin-headlamp front end that had been warmly received when it had been pioneered on the CLK Concept car in 1993. However, the attempt to match the oval headlamps by designing ovals into the rear light lenses was not a success. The rest of the

styling was curvaceous and very different from the rather upright W124s, but was still instantly recognizable as coming from the Mercedes stable. The W210s brought better aerodynamics, too: the Cd of the first models ranged between 0.27 and 0.29.

Equipment levels also followed the new Mercedes policy. Instead of a basic model on which almost everything was an extra-cost option, there were the same three trim levels that had been seen on the W202 C class: Classic, Elegance and Avantgarde. Identifying badges were added to the bump strip on the front wings. Even the most basic Classic models had ABS, traction control, ESP, twin airbags, seat-belt pre-tensioners and force limiters, electric windows front and rear, an outside temperature gauge, a pollen filter, a third brake light, and cupholders in the rear centre armrest. New options – standard on some models – included side airbags in the doors, Xenon headlamps with a self-dipping feature, speed-

This 1995 car shows the alloy wheels associated with higher trim levels than the entry-level Classic (see above). In this case, the car has the Elegance specification.

sensitive and rain-sensing wipers, and Parktronic parking sensors. A 65-litre fuel tank was standard, but it was possible to order an 80-litre alternative, which of course ate into the boot space on saloons.

Classic was the entry-level specification, and brought cloth upholstery and 15-in steel wheels (which were also standard on all the first diesel-engined W210s). The Elegance models had ten-hole alloy wheels, chrome on

Specification levels were revealed by discreet badges on the front wings. The Elegance badge…

… and the Sport badge from an E430.

the door handles and bumpers, and chrome on the bump strips, which were distinctively coloured in grey. They had extra equipment, and wood veneer inside. The Avantgarde models had Sport suspension as standard, with 16in five-hole alloys running on wide tyres. They were distinguished on the outside by black B-pillars, blue-tinted heat-absorbing glass with a grey shade band across the top of the windscreen, and a grille with five black-painted bars and one in chrome. Xenon head-lamps were standard and the interior trim was flashier.

As for the estates, they retained the self-levelling suspension and self-closing tailgate that had been much liked on their W124 predecessors. A rearward-facing third row of seats was again optional, and this folded down into the floor to provide a flat load space when necessary – 985 litres (34cu ft) with the

second-row seats in use, and 1975 litres (70cu ft) with them folded down. Some customers complained that the more angled rear profile of the W210 reduced load-space versatility in comparison with the nearly vertical rear end of the W124, and did not like the fact that there was only a single underfloor locker instead of the two in the older model.

There was of course no pleasing some people, and Mercedes customers had traditionally been very conservative in their outlook. But there was also no denying that the cost-saving that had been so important to Stuttgart was apparent in small details: the doors shut without the solid thunk so characteristic of older Mercedes; the traditional oil-pressure gauge had been replaced by a simple warning light; there was no damper on the ash-tray; and there was a lack of solidity about the otherwise beautifully designed dashboard. In addition,

The E430 with its 279PS 4.3-litre V8 arrived as a 1997 model. This is a 2001 car with US specification.

As was by now customary with Mercedes-Benz, the estate versions of the 210 range had been designed alongside the saloons. As a result, their styling was just as elegant, with no suggestion that the rear upper body section had simply been added to an existing design.

when the cars went on sale, there were a number of build-quality issues which took the company several years to sort out.

The First Cars

The new E class was announced in June 1995 with a range of nine engines that covered every option, from taxi to executive hot-rod. There were five petrol engines and four diesels, most being carry-overs from the W124 range, although uprated to a greater or lesser extent.

The petrol-engined models started with the four-cylinder E200, which now had 134bhp and hot-film air mass metering; next up was the E230, with a big-bore version of the old 2.2-litre engine, which delivered the same power but more torque than the engine it replaced. It also had a stiffer block, to reduce

noise and vibration levels. To be fair, neither of these engines was very exciting and both were outclassed by rivals from BMW and Audi, although both were competent enough for traditional Mercedes customers. The petrol sixes came in the E280 and E320, both having the M104 24-valve motors that had powered the W124 range. Then there was a new top model, designed to take sales away from BMW's V8-powered 5 Series. This was the E420, with the 4.2-litre V8 from the S class. Announced in June 1995 but not available until February 1996, it was not made available in every market, and the UK was one of those that missed out.

As for the diesels, all were four-valve types with indirect injection. The two five-cylinder types, the 113PS E250 Diesel and the 129PS E290 Turbodiesel did not make it to the UK. However, the 95PS four-cylinder E220 Diesel

The 3-litre diesel engine was available in both naturally aspirated and turbocharged forms. To distinguish one model from the other, the turbocharged model wore a full set of badges describing it as an E300 Turbodiesel.

and the 136PS six-cylinder E300 Diesel did reach the UK, and were well received there.

As usual, production of right-hand-drive cars lagged a little behind that of left-hand-drive cars; this was one reason why the UK did not get the E280 until the end of 1996 and also had to wait until the new year for the estate models. However, the range was not yet complete even in Germany, and the high-performance flagship from AMG was not announced until January 1997.

The flagship was the E50 AMG, a replacement for the hot-rod E500 of the old W124 line-up but a car that was deliberately more 'mainstream' in its approach and its marketing. At its heart was AMG's 347PS development of the M119 5-litre V8, featuring new camshafts and inlet valves. There was also a big-bore exhaust, a special air filter and, of course, different ECU settings for both the engine and the standard automatic gearbox. The suspension featured stiffer dampers, stronger anti-roll bars, shorter springs and stiffer bushes, while the front brake discs had a larger diameter than the standard W210 types. Steering was more direct, too.

Of course, the AMG car had to be easily recognizable, but it was in line with Mercedes' latest thinking (and with its cost-saving policies) that it was nowhere near as different from the standard W210 as the old E500 had been from the mainstream W124. Distinguishing features were round foglights in the front bumper, special sills, cut-outs in the rear apron for the twin exhausts, special 18in wheels and, of course, a lowered stance. For owners and enthusiasts, though, the car's key features were its sharpened handling and its ability to accelerate to 100km/h from rest in just 6.2 seconds. Top speed, as usual, was limited to 250km/h. None of these AMG models made it to the UK.

The 1998-model W210s were introduced over the summer of 1997, and included one new model – an 88PS E200 Diesel, which would only ever be sold in Portugal. Production of the original E220 Diesel stopped, and the car reappeared for the taxi market with its engine modified to run on bio-diesel, and with power down to 75PS from the earlier 95PS. The engine of the petrol E200 was modified with a variable inlet camshaft,

The US market was a very important one for the W210s. This is a 2001-model estate variant, known to US buyers as the 'wagon'.

The 4MATIC system had originally been developed to give extra traction for customers in the Alpine regions of Europe, but it was introduced to the USA as well in the wake of Audi's success with four-wheel-drive models. This overhead view shows the layout of the system.

which gave no more power but did improve the engine's torque spread at higher speeds. The engine-management system of the E280 was also upgraded. But perhaps the most far-reaching change was to the automatic trans-missions. All the four-speed types that had been available on the first cars were replaced by new five-speed types with electronic con-trol systems. Improvements were seen in both refinement and economy. The five-speed auto-matic became standard on all petrol and diesel six-cylinder models except the petrol E280.

New V6s and V8s

The 1997 Geneva Show provided the show-case for the next set of changes. The new Brake Assist System (BAS), which recognized the signs of an emergency stop and automatically applied full braking power, was an important introduction. as was the Active Service System (ASSYST), a service interval indicator that worked by analysing the condition of the engine oil. There were new models, too. The

diesel range was reinforced by the addition of an E300 Turbodiesel with the 177PS engine from the S class, and the first 4MATIC variants (sold mainly in the Alpine regions of southern Europe) also became available. Based on the E280 and E320, these both had the five-speed automatic transmission as standard, driving to a new permanent four-wheel-drive system, which had been developed with the help of Steyr-Daimler-Puch. This could now be inter-rupted – in effect, switched to two-wheel drive – electronically by the ETS traction con-trol system.

The biggest news, though, related to the arrival of new V6 and V8 petrol engines. The two designs were closely related and shared a number of components. Both the M112 V6 and the M113 V8 had a 90-degree angle between the cylinder banks (ideal for a V8, less so for a V6), with two inlet valves and a single exhaust valve. This element of the design had resulted largely from Mercedes' desire to save manufacturing costs. Both engines also had twin ignition systems, and were lighter and

All the interest of the 4MATIC system lay at the front of the car, drive to the rear wheels being the same as on standard models. This picture shows in detail the unique features of a 4MATIC system on a W210.

more fuel-efficient than the engines they were destined to replace.

The first of these new engines to appear in the showrooms were the 2.8-litre in the E280 and the long-stroke 3.2-litre in the E320, in each case replacing the straight-six engine in the earlier car of the same name. Confusingly, perhaps, both engines had exactly the same swept volume as the engines they replaced. However, each was claimed to be 25 per cent lighter than its M104 equivalent, and there were slight increases in top-end power, although not in torque.

Stuttgart's strategy became clearer still at the Frankfurt Show in September, when a third V6 engine, this time with a reduced bore size and the short stroke of the 2.8-litre type, arrived in the E240 models. These immediately replaced the four-cylinder E230 in most countries, delivering a six-cylinder model to match the six-cylinder BMW 523i and thus strengthening Mercedes' presence in a crucial area of the market. In practice, however, the E230 remained available until June 1998 in some countries and for CKD assembly.

The Frankfurt Show also witnessed the introduction of the first M113 V8 engines in the E class, when the E430 replaced the old M119-powered E420 and the E55 AMG

replaced the E50 AMG. In fact, AMG had made no secret of the fact that they were not very impressed by the new three-valve engine, but, as that was all Stuttgart was prepared to supply them, they made the best of it and squeezed 354PS out of the engine by enlarging both the bore and stroke of the 4.2-litre type.

There were yet more new models in this flurry of activity at the start of the 1998 model-year. Greece, Italy and Portugal were treated to a new E250 Turbodiesel model with 150PS and a five-speed manual gearbox as the only transmission option, while other markets were offered the E200 Kompressor – the first E class to be fitted with a supercharger. Although the M111 four-cylinder petrol engine was essentially the same as that in the existing E200, the addition of the supercharger made a big difference. It boosted power from 136PS to 192PS, and took torque from 190Nm to 270Nm while giving a greater and more useable spread across the engine's rev range as well. Acceleration was transformed, the 0–100km/h sprint time reducing from 12.3 seconds to 8.9 seconds, but buyers paid a small penalty in increased fuel consumption. Sixteen-inch wheels with 215/55 tyres were specified as standard to cope with this extra performance.

The Common-Rail Diesels

In this period, Mercedes were quite clearly pedalling very hard to catch up with their arch-rivals at BMW, and 1997 also saw the arrival of a 'show special', which gave advance warning of new technology. Based on an E class saloon and badged as an E400 CDI, it had an all-alloy 4-litre twin-turbo V8 diesel engine (which stole some of the thunder of BMW's new diesel V8), featuring high-pressure common-rail fuel injection. The car never went into production, although the engine did go into the new W220 S class in 2000 and of course the

ABOVE: The V8-powered E430 was not an AMG model, but it could be equipped with a variety of AMG options. This one has the lower ride height, alloy wheels, and the special front apron and sills.

RIGHT: A proud owner would always want to display an AMG badge on the boot lid, too!

ABOVE: Special wheels and sill panels mark out this 2001 US model on an E55 AMG.

LEFT: The top model from the W210 range was the E55 AMG, and its heart was the AMG-prepared V8 engine of 5.5 litres. The under-bonnet view is of a 1998 car.

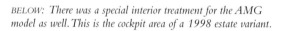

BELOW: There was a special interior treatment for the AMG model as well. This is the cockpit area of a 1998 estate variant.

common-rail technology would be a feature of all future Mercedes passenger-car diesels.

The first common-rail diesels available through the showrooms were introduced in June 1998 for the 1999 season. The new technology was applied to the smaller diesel-engined models, where new OM611 four-cylinder engines were introduced. These new engines were also turbocharged and intercooled, although the designations of the models they powered did not reflect the fact. Their turbochargers used the latest variable turbine geometry, to reduce turbo lag and give optimum boost right across the rev range.

In fact, at this stage there was just one new engine capacity, of 2151cc, but Mercedes managed to make two new models out of it by the cost-effective method of providing each with a different engine-management system. The E200 CDI had 102PS, while the E220 CDI boasted 125PS. The smaller-engined car replaced the old export-only E200 Diesel, but was in fact made available in all of Mercedes' diesel markets. The new engines were

---

Best Buys

Various factors can influence purchase costs from time to time, and it is not possible to take these into account here. However, in terms of practicality and enjoyment, these are the best W210 E class models to buy.

The high-performance diesel engine came of age during the period of the W210s' manufacture, and it is no surprise that the best all-rounders in the range are the later diesels. An E220 CDI makes an excellent buy for high-mileage or everyday family use, while the strong performance and good fuel economy of the E320 CDI mean that for many users it will be the very best option.

Although the early four-cylinder petrol models were really outclassed by rivals from BMW and Audi almost as soon as they were launched, the later V6s are a much better bet. For really high performance, an E55 AMG is obviously the car to go for, but realistically an E430 is nearly as much fun, as well as being cheaper to run. Quite obviously, fuel economy will not be anywhere near as good as the figures quoted on pages 105–6 if the V8-powered cars are regularly used to their maximum potential!

A reshaped front apron and indicator repeaters in the door mirrors were two obvious features of the 2000 model-year facelift. By the time this car was new in 2001, silver had become one of the most popular colours in European markets, and this press photograph of an E320 CDI reflected the fact.

extremely well received, not least because of their smooth power delivery, their high torque which delivered excellent acceleration, and their low exhaust emissions.

Mid-Life Facelift

The W210s were facelifted in mid-1999, just four years after their introduction. This was a clear indication that the range was to have a shorter life-span than had been usual for past Mercedes; the W124 models had waited nearly twice as long before getting their significant facelift.

In fact, the facelift was quite subtle. The front end featured narrower headlamps (more akin to those on the CLK models) and a new apron spoiler with a gaping 'mouth', which was perhaps the most easily recognizable feature. Sharp eyes would also have spotted that the panels covering the headlamp washers were now squarer than before. The remodelled front end was one reason why the facelifted cars were 23mm (just under an inch) longer than the outgoing models. The most obvious (and welcome) rear-end change was a more conventional rear-light lens design, which did away with the awkward oval section. The re-shaped door mirrors now incorporated

The later W210 models had indicator repeaters in the door mirrors, in line with the new Mercedes family look. None of that stopped the mirror bodies taking the usual battering from insects and road debris, though, as this picture shows!

a turn indicator repeater like that introduced the previous year on the W220 S class.

Inside the cars, a key difference was the new multi-function steering wheel, with a larger display screen on the dash. Automatics took on the new manual control introduced on the W220.

The model range evolved, too. There were two new common-rail diesel models – the

The darker colour seen in this publicity shot of a post-facelift saloon arguably sets off its lines much better than the popular silver.

ABOVE: The estates were facelifted in the same way as the saloons in July 1999. This one is wearing one of the new alloy wheel options that arrived at the same time.

RIGHT: As was traditional for Mercedes by this stage, the engine bay was tidily presented, with separate compartments for the battery and other items not driven directly from the engine itself. This is a 2001 four-cylinder E200 Kompressor, a model available only in certain European countries.

How Fast? How Thirsty?

These figures are typical for W210 E class models, but variations in the car's equipment levels and load, and variations in driving style will cause differences that may be significant.

	0–60mph	Max speed	Mpg (overall)
E220 CDI	10.4secs (manual)	211km/h (132mph)	45 (6.3ltr/100km)
E230	8.9secs	210km/h (131mph)	25 (11.3ltr/100km)
E240	9.6secs (manual)	221km/h (138mph)	27.5 (10.3ltr/100km)
E270 CDI	9.5secs (manual)	213km/h (133mph)	39 (7.25ltr/100km)
E280 (V6)	9.1secs (auto)	230km/h (143mph)	32 (8.8ltr/100km)
E320 (in-line)	7.8secs (auto)	233km/h (146mph)	22 (12.8ltr/100km)
E320 CDI	8.3secs	230km/h (143mph)	35 (8ltr/100km)
E430	6.6secs	250km/h (155mph) (restricted)	26 (10.8ltr/100km)
E55 AMG	5.7secs	250km/h (155mph) (restricted)	23 (12.3ltr/100km)

five-cylinder E270 CDI with 170PS and the six-cylinder E320 CDI with 197PS – and the four-cylinder E220 CDI was uprated from 125PS to 143PS. An E280 estate was introduced at long last, the only estate model with this engine having been the 4MATIC type until this point. A 4MATIC version of the E430 was added to the range, and then a few months after the main model changes came the introduction of an E55 AMG 4MATIC, which was always destined to be a rare car. Both these V8-engined 4MATIC models had to use an older version of the five-speed automatic transmission, as the latest version was too big for the space available within the body shell.

In this guise, the W210 range continued into the first quarter of 2002, when production of the saloons was discontinued on a model-by-model basis to make way for the new W211 E class. The estates remained in production for some 12 months longer, the final examples being built in the spring of 2003.

Specifications for W210 Models

Engines

Petrol saloons

E200	1998cc M111 4-cyl, 136PS & 190Nm	(1995–2000)
	1998cc M111 4-cyl, 163PS & 230Nm	(2000–2002)
E200 Kompressor	1998cc M111 4-cyl, 192PS & 270Nm	(1997–2000)
E230	2295cc M111 4-cyl, 150PS & 220Nm	(1995–1998)
E240	2398cc M112 V6, 170PS & 225Nm	(1997–2000)
	2398cc M112 V6, 170PS & 240Nm	(2000–2002)
E280	2799cc M104 6-cyl, 193PS & 270Nm	(1995–1997)
	2799cc M112 V6, 204PS & 270Nm	(1997–2002)
E320	3199cc M104 6-cyl, 220PS & 315Nm	(1995–1997)
	3199cc M112 V6, 224PS & 315Nm	(1997–2002)
E420	4196cc M119 V8, 279PS & 400Nm	(1996–1998)
E430	4266cc M113 V8, 279PS & 400Nm	(1997–2002)
E50 AMG	4973cc M119 V8, 347PS & 480Nm	(1996–1997)
E55 AMG	5439cc M113 V8, 354PS & 530Nm	(1997–2002)

Diesel saloons

E200 Diesel	1997cc OM604 4-cyl, 88PS & 135Nm	(1996–1998)
E200 CDI	2151cc OM611 4-cyl, 102PS & 235Nm	(1998–1999)
	2148cc OM611 4-cyl, 116PS & 250Nm	(1999–2002)
E220 Diesel	2155cc OM604 4-cyl, 95PS & 150Nm	(1995–1999)
	Bio-diesel-ready version with 75 PS	
E220 CDI	2151cc OM611 4-cyl, 125PS & 300Nm	(1998–1999)
	2148cc OM611 4-cyl, 143PS & 315Nm	(1999–2002)
E250 Diesel	2497cc OM605 4-cyl, 113PS & 170Nm	(1995–1999)
E250 Turbodiesel	2497cc OM605 4-cyl, 150PS & 280Nm	(1995–1999)
E270 CDI	2685cc OM612 5-cyl, 170PS & 370Nm	(1999–2002)
	400Nm on automatic models	
E290 Turbodiesel	2874cc OM602 5-cyl, 129PS & 300Nm	(1995–1999)
E300 Diesel	2996cc OM 606 6-cyl, 136PS & 210Nm	(1995–1997)
E300 Turbodiesel	2996cc OM 606 6-cyl, 177PS & 210Nm	(1997–1999)
E320 CDI	3222cc OM613 6-cyl, 197PS & 470Nm	(1999–2002)

continued overleaf

Specifications for W210 Models *continued*

Engines *continued*

Petrol estates

E200	1998cc M111 4-cyl, 136PS & 190Nm	(1996–2000)
E200 Kompressor	1998cc M111 4-cyl, 192PS & 270Nm	(1997–2000)
	1998cc M111 4-cyl, 163PS & 230Nm	(2000–2002)
E230	2295cc M111 4-cyl, 150PS & 220Nm	(1996–1998)
E240	2398cc M112 V6, 170PS & 225Nm	(1997–2000)
	2597cc M112 V6, 170PS & 240Nm	(2000–2002)
E280	2799cc M112 V6, 204PS & 270Nm	(1999–2003)
E320	3199cc M112 V6, 224PS & 315Nm	(1997–2003)

Diesel estates

E220 CDI	2151cc OM611 4-cyl, 125PS & 300Nm	(1998–1999)
	2148cc OM611 4-cyl, 143PS & 315Nm	(1999–2003)
E250 Diesel	2497cc OM605 4-cyl, 113PS & 170Nm	(1996–1999)
E250 Turbodiesel	2497cc OM605 4-cyl, 150PS & 280Nm	(1997–1999)
E270 CDI	2685cc OM612 5-cyl, 170PS & 370Nm	(1999–2002)
	400Nm on automatic models	
E290 Turbodiesel	2874cc OM602 5-cyl, 129PS & 300Nm	(1996–1999)
E300 Turbodiesel	2996cc OM 606 6-cyl, 177PS & 210Nm	(1997–1999)
E320 CDI	3222cc OM613 6-cyl, 197PS & 470Nm	(1999–2003)

Transmissions

Five-speed manual (to 1999)
Six-speed manual (from 1999)
Four-speed automatic (to 1996)
Five-speed automatic (from 1996)

Running gear

Front suspension with twin wishbones, coil springs, gas dampers and anti-roll bar.
Rear suspension with five links, coil springs, gas dampers and anti-roll bar. Hydropneumatic self-levelling optional.

Dimensions

Wheelbase: 2833mm (112in); 3570mm (140in) (all long-wheelbase models)
Front track: 1528–1542mm (60–61in), depending on model and tyre choice
Rear track: 1528–1543mm (60–61in), depending on model and tyre choice

Length: 4795mm (189in) (saloons to 1999); 4818mm (190in) (saloons from 1999); 4816mm (190in) (estates to 1999); 4839mm (190in) (estates from 1999); 5553mm (219in) (long-wheelbase models to 1999); 5576mm (220in) (long-wheelbase models from 1999)
Width: 1799mm (71in)
Height: 1411–1441mm (56–57in), depending on model and tyre choice

Weights (typical)

E200 saloon to 1999:	1940kg (4268lb)
E200 Kompressor saloon:	2010kg (4422lb)
E280 V6 saloon:	2070kg (4554lb)
E280 saloon with in-line six:	2100kg (4620lb)
E320 CDI saloon:	2160kg (4752lb)
E55 AMG and E430 saloons:	2210kg (4862lb)
E240 V6 estate:	2250kg (4950lb)
E250 Turbodiesel estate:	2260kg (4972lb)
E220 CDI estate:	2270kg (4994lb)

7 The Revolutionary A Class

The two Oil Crises of the 1970s caused car manufacturers around the world to begin serious studies of small and economical cars for city use. At Mercedes, the first results of this were shown in public in 1982 in the shape of a car known as the NAFA (its initials represent the German words for 'travel for short distances'). With a 40bhp rear-mounted three-cylinder engine, this car weighed just 750kg (1650lb) and had an overall length of just 2.5m – and in fact it had a number of interesting similarities to the Smart car that went on sale in 1998.

However, worries about the cost of oil gradually receded, and by 1986 Stuttgart decided that the time for such a small car to wear the Mercedes badge had not yet arrived. The NAFA project was officially abandoned.

The whole point of the A class was that it was primarily a city car, and this 1997 press picture showed it in the urban setting where it was expected to be most at home. It was nevertheless a more than capable long-distance cruiser, too.

The first publicity pictures had already been issued when the A class handling issue arose. This one dates from 1997, and shows the three different trim levels available at the launch: Classic, Elegance and Avantgarde.

Within three years a project team was once again looking at a small city car, however. This new car was larger than the NAFA, and this time its three-cylinder engine was mounted at the front and driving the front wheels.

One of the problems that the Mercedes engineers had encountered in designing their city car was that of maintaining the marque's traditional levels of crash protection. In a short car with its engine ahead of the passenger compartment, there was almost no bodywork that could be used as a crumple zone to absorb the forces of the collision. The problem called for a revolutionary solution, which was found in 'sandwich' construction.

'Sandwich' construction set the floor of the passenger compartment above the underside of the monocoque, leaving a space between the two into which the engine would be pushed in the case of a frontal impact. This ensured that the engine could not penetrate into the passenger compartment, and so the major hazard of frontal collisions was avoided. 'Sandwich' construction was first seen in public in the Vision A concept car that Mercedes displayed at the 1993 Frankfurt Motor Show. The letter A showed that this was intended as an entry-level Mercedes, below the compact C class, the medium-sized E class and the large S class. However, in 1993 the new model designations were so new that probably very few people recognized the significance of that letter A!

The year 1993 was of course a significant one for Mercedes, when its top management changed and brought in a new vision of the brand's future. However, it was really the very positive reaction provoked by the Vision A at Frankfurt that ensured that there would be a small car called the A class within that vision. Work soon began on project W168, drawing on all the ideas that had gone into the Vision A and into the NAFA car.

For Mercedes, the A class demanded a real revolution in thinking, and the clever 'sandwich' construction was just the start. It was very much smaller, and was intended to be very much cheaper, than any previous model to wear the three-pointed star. The compact dimensions demanded front-wheel-drive, as seen in the Vision A, which made this the very first Mercedes to have such a driveline configuration. Its development also required a new family of engines, which would be mounted transversely to save space; this was yet another new departure for the company. Other space-saving ideas included an electronic servo to give power assistance to the steering, and to make city driving easier there was to be a clutchless semi-automatic transmission option. Small wonder, then, that, by the time the A class was announced, in 1997, it had cost nearly £1 billion to develop.

It was a massive gamble for Stuttgart, and the company took no chances. Billboard advertisements began to appear about a year

Interior shots of the three trim levels show how variations in materials were used to achieve the desired effects. From the left: Avantgarde, Classic and Elegance interiors.

before the launch to familiarize the public with the idea of a new, smaller Mercedes. The press launch was staged in Belgium in June and July 1997, and journalists scurried back to their word processors to eulogize the revolutionary thinking that had gone into the car and to prepare the public for another new success from Mercedes. The only murmurs of discontent related to the rather plasticky interior and to somewhat soggy handling on the entry-level Classic and mid-range Elegance models. The A class was a natural choice for the finalists in the annual European Car of the Year contest, and there can have been few who did not expect it to win.

Unfortunately, things did not turn out like that. Within days of full production production starting at Mercedes' Rastatt plant (which it did on 15 October), the Car of the Year jury put it and every other contender through a double-lane-swerve manoeuvre in Denmark. The A class lifted a wheel on the second swerve. Inevitably, this led to great consterna-

tion (although it could not be persuaded to repeat the performance).

In Sweden, the magazine *Teknikens Värld* picked up on this, and determined to see if the A class was as unstable as this result suggested. On 21 October, journalist Robert Collin put the car through a double-swerve manoeuvre around some cones – and the A class rolled over, injuring one of the passengers in the car. All over Europe, other magazines had already planned similar tests, and of the nineteen that carried them out within the next few weeks, two made the A class lift a wheel, and three rolled it. None of the cars that rolled had the stiffer suspension that was standard on the Avantgarde model and optional on the Classic and Elegance types.

The news of the first, Swedish, rollover reached the Mercedes-Benz Board in Tokyo on 22 October, where they were proudly launching the new Maybach limousine. The stunned Board held an emergency meeting, issued a bland statement to the press, which

was obliged to start work on a new factory to cope with the anticipated volumes. Meanwhile, some 300 engineers at Stuttgart worked round-the-clock to re-engineer the suspension (despite the TV statement by the company's Board members) and to get it ready for production.

By early November, the job had been done. The ride height of the A class had been lowered, and it sat 42mm (1.5in) lower at the front and 22mm (just under an inch) lower at the rear than the original Classic and Elegance models. It had wider, lower-profile Michelin tyres, a wider rear track, stiffer anti-roll bars, revised steering geometry to increase understeer, firmer springs, new dampers and, of course, ESP. On 10 November, Mercedes took a newly modified A class to the racing circuit at Jerez, engaged former Formula 1 World Champion Niki Lauda to come and drive the car, and invited along Robert Collin and representatives of the three German magazines which had repeated the rollover accident. Everyone pronounced themselves satisfied with the changes: the car was safe.

The good news was rushed to Stuttgart, and on 11 November deliveries of the A class were suspended. The revisions were announced in public, and the owners of all 2500 cars that had so far been sold were contacted and offered the loan of a C class until their cars could be modified to the new production standard. It was a measure of their satisfaction with the A class that fewer than 10 per cent actually took up the offer! Orders began to come in again: Mercedes had taken 100,000 orders before the reports of the first rollover accident became public, when new orders had almost completely dried up and 4000 existing orders had been cancelled.

However, the nightmare was not yet over for Mercedes. In order to meet production targets, they had no option but to continue building cars to the original specification at Rastatt until everything was in place for production of the revised models in February 1998. Some 17,000 cars would have to be stockpiled and

stated (accurately) that they had no knowledge of a problem with the A class, and immediately arranged for a task force to be established at Stuttgart to investigate the rollovers and to report on the problem. There was much burning of the midnight oil at Stuttgart, and on 29 October Jürgen Hubbert and Jürgen Schrempp made a live statement on German television. They said that there were no plans to change the car's suspension, and pointed out that the double-swerve manoeuvre which had caused the rollovers was unrealistic. However, they did plan to change the Goodyear tyres on the car for the alternative Michelins (which were fitted with the stiffer suspension and gave a lower ride height), and they would fit ESP as standard.

ESP had been planned for introduction as an option on the A class in late 1998, so its test programme was brought forward. This in itself caused a massive amount of work for Mercedes engineers; ESP manufacturer Bosch had not planned on such demand for the system, and then modified before going out through the dealerships. The whole exercise cost the company an estimated £110 million. Worse, precautionary testing during December on the Smart micro-car, in which Mercedes had a major interest, showed that this, too, had a rollover problem. An urgent redesign was put in hand, delaying the launch of the Smart by around six months and costing MCC – the company set up jointly by Mercedes and Swatch to make the Smart – a further large sum of money.

Mercedes could not afford to get the relaunch of the A class wrong, so 400 journalists were invited to the Goodyear test track at Mireval in France and encouraged to put pre-production versions of the revised A class through double-swerve manoeuvres, and more, to see if they could turn it over. The company no doubt held its breath – although it had retained enough sense of humour to present every journalist with a stuffed model of an elk in honour of the so-called 'elk test', which had originally caused the rollover. (The Swedes themselves never called it the 'elk test',

but the double-swerve manoeuvre had been devised by them to replicate a driver's likely reaction to an errant elk, a not uncommon sight on Swedish roads.)

Everything went according to plan. Nobody managed to roll the revised A class, although some journalists tried very hard indeed. Stuttgart breathed a collective sign of relief and gave the final go-ahead to production of the revised models (which began on 9 February) and to the programme to modify all cars built to the original specification. The A class had definitively reached the market, just over three months behind schedule.

The First Cars

The A class was certainly a remarkable machine in engineering terms, although to many long-standing fans of the marque it did not look or feel like a traditional Mercedes. Its one-box design was very different from the conventional three-box style of Stuttgart's bigger saloons, and even a version of the Mercedes 'sports'-style grille at the front was not initial-

The three 'standard' trim levels were by no means the only ones, of course. From 1998, Mercedes introduced its 'designo' option (note the supposedly modern lower-case initial letter!) for the A class as well, allowing customers to specify more or less what they wanted inside the car – at a cost, of course.

This early press picture of the new A class shows how the first cars looked. The 'RA' on the number-plate stands for Rastatt, home of the factory where the model was built.

ly convincing. The quirky rear side window design – actually a clever solution which combined structural strength with adequate light for the passenger compartment – was a major stumbling-block for some observers, too, as was the rather plasticky feel of the dashboard and other interior trim items.

There was, however, no argument over the clever use of interior space. As early as the Frankfurt Show, in September 1995, Mercedes had displayed an Interior Concept for the car to keep up the momentum started by the Vision A concept two years earlier. Recognizing that there was insufficient luggage space in the original Vision A, the Mercedes engineers had lengthened the whole car by 225mm (9in). However, an important part of the concept was interior flexibility, allowing for different ways of using the space by folding or removing seats in the fashion associated with MPVs. In the end, no fewer than seventy-two different seat and luggage-space configurations were available within the tiny 3575mm (141in) overall length of the A class.

As adopted for production, the A class interior gave 390 litres (nearly 14 cu ft) of 'boot' space behind the seats and a maximum of 1740 litres (61.5 cu ft) of carrying capacity when all seats except the driver's were removed. The significance of that figure becomes more apparent when it is put into context: the load-carrying capacity of this very small car was greater than that of the contemporary C class estates (1510 litres/53 cu ft), and fell mid-way between them and the contemporary W210 E class estates, which had a maximum of 1975 litres (70 cu ft).

Even more remarkable, perhaps, was Mercedes' claim that the A class offered levels of passive safety equivalent to those of the much larger E class cars. So, although an observer's perception might have been that the driver and front passenger sat dangerously close to the nose of the car, the fact was that clever construction and, of course, airbags, protected them from the worst effects of a collision. Part of the structural strength of the A class lay in that revolutionary 'sandwich' construction, of course, but the need to achieve

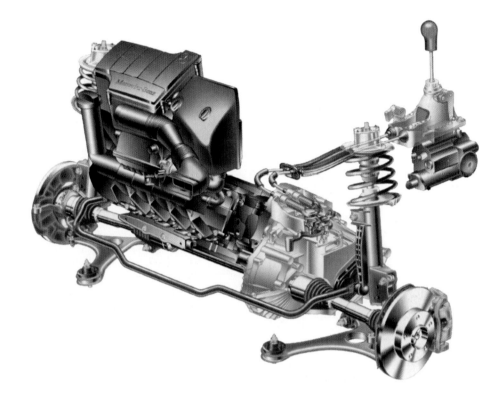

ABOVE: *Transverse engines were new to Mercedes-Benz models, as was so much else on the A class. This picture shows the layout of the front suspension and the cable-operated gearchange linkage.*

LEFT: *The new engines included diesels – or, rather, one diesel in two states of tune. This picture of the A170 CDI engine is taken from the rear right-hand side, and shows how far the cylinder block was canted forwards.*

114

high levels of crashworthiness had forced the Mercedes engineers to go even further and develop some novel solutions. One of these was an aluminium front section with 'crash boxes' that bolted to the longitudinal side members. After a collision, this was simple to unbolt and replace, saving on workshop times and costs.

Right from the start, it had been obvious that no existing Mercedes engines would be suitable for the new car, so two new families of compact four-cylinder engines were developed for the transverse installation that the A class needed. Mercedes claimed that they were 25 per cent lighter than any other existing production four-cylinder engines of the same capacity.

The petrol engines were the new M166 types, with swept volumes of 1.4 litres and 1.6 litres, delivering 82PS for the A140 and 102 PS for the A160. The diesels were turbocharged four-valve types with common-rail direct injection, and carried the OM668 designation. Of great technical interest was their all-alloy design; most diesels of the time still used iron cylinder blocks, and these new engines were a clear indication of the way Mercedes diesel design would go. There was a single 1.7-litre size, from which the engineers created two different engines by the simple expedient of adding an intercooler to one of them. As a result, for the A160 CDI model there was a 60 PS power output, while the intercooled engine gave 90 PS for the A170 CDI derivative.

Transmissions were new, too, and the standard gearbox was a compact five-speed manual type: the SG150 for the entry-level cars and the SG 180 for the more powerful models. As planned, this could be ordered at extra cost with an automatic clutch, in which case the transmission was known as the ACS type (the letters standing for Automatic Clutch System, and becoming AKS in Germany). In all cases, the differential for the front-wheel drive was integral with the gearbox. However, it would not be long before a proper automatic trans-

---

Twin-Engined Specials

In November 1998, a pair of very special A class cars broke cover. They were the brainchild of W168 project leader Ulrich Bruhnke, who presented them to Formula 1 World Champion Mika Häkkinen and his team-mate David Coulthard.

The two cars were each fitted with a pair of 1.9-litre engines, one in the standard location at the front and the other at the rear. The two engines could be run in tandem through an automatic clutch system, to give a total of 250PS, or the rear engine could be shut down independently. The maximum speed of these cars was reported to be 230km/h (143mph), and the 0–60mph acceleration time was 5.7 seconds.

The cars were fitted with 18-in wheels and 255/35 tyres; the wheel arches had to be extended by some 10mm (just under half an inch) to cover these. There were disc brakes and the rear and the front ventilated discs came from an AMG E55 model.

---

mission was added to the options list. The W5A 180 five-speed gearbox with electronic control and sequential Tipfunction over-ride control was announced as an option for the A140, A160 and A170 CDI in July 1998. It immediately attracted attention within the motor industry as the shortest and lightest five-speed automatic gearbox then in production anywhere in the world.

There was more technical interest in the power-assisted steering, which was powered electrically rather than driven by belt from the engine in the traditional manner. This, claimed Stuttgart, reduced the power drain on the engine and therefore contributed to better fuel economy. As for the wheels and tyres, the standard entry-level combination on these first cars (after the February 1998 revisions) was a 15-in steel rim with 195/50 tyres. However, a selection of extra-cost alloy wheels was also made available, and there were 16in and 17in sizes with 205/45 tyres for the former and 205/40 tyres for the latter.

In common with other Mercedes ranges, the A class was made available with different trim levels. It had three: Classic was the entry-level; next up was Elegance, which brought alloy wheels plus colour-coding of the door mirrors, grille and door handles; Avantgarde was the top specification, adding to the Elegance equipment some exterior fittings and lower-profile tyres.

Expanding the Range

Fortunately, the 'elk test' fiasco was quickly forgotten, and Mercedes found themselves with another best-seller on their hands. However, the A class had been designed as an essentially practical car, and there was nothing in the range to appeal to enthusiasts. There had been plans to develop a high-performance derivative from quite early on, when Mercedes spokesmen had spoken of the possibility of an eventual AMG model. That, in the end, did not materialize because AMG found that they could not get the performance they wanted from the M166 engine. However, more

powerful and more sporting variants of the A class did reach the showrooms over the next few years.

Part of the marketing offensive was an optional five-speed 'sports' gearbox, introduced as an extra-cost option in September 1999 on all models. However, more noticeable, in the showrooms at least, was the new A190 model, which was announced some three months before that. Its engine, a long-stroke, big-bore version of the existing M166 four-cylinder, developed 125PS. The standard gearbox was the new five-speed 'sports' manual, but a five-speed automatic was an option right from the beginning.

The A190 promised an astonishing top speed of 197km/h (123mph), so Stuttgart's engineers had had to improve its braking system in order to cope. At the rear, the existing models' drums were replaced by discs, while the front discs were replaced by ventilated discs with a larger diameter. To make room for these, the standard wheel size was increased from 15in to 16in. Only Elegance and Avantgarde trim levels were available, Classic

The rear view was arguably the least successful aspect of the A class, although this carefully taken publicity picture makes it look quite elegant!

presumably being viewed as too down-market for a buyer who might want this top model of the A class range. However, the body kit of lower front apron and more 'sporty' body-coloured side sills that came with the new engine was perhaps not the A190's greatest success, as it tended to make the car look short and dumpy.

No car manufacturer, of course, can work independently of legislation, and changes in European exhaust emissions regulations obliged Stuttgart to make quite a major change further down the range in June 2000. The problem was with the A140 automatic, which pumped out more noxious emissions from its tailpipe than new regulations would allow. The only way to get around this was to fit the larger 1.6-litre version of the engine, as used in the A160 automatic, which obviously did not have to work as hard to deliver the required performance. However, scrapping the A140 automatic was not seen as an option: it would have seemed as if Mercedes were moving the A class up-market. The A140 automatic remained on sale, but from this point it had a 1.6-litre engine that put out the same 82PS as the old 1.4-litre, with rather more torque. The manual A140 meanwhile remained unchanged.

There were further minor tweaks to the range in September 1999. All models received firmer seats, and Elegance derivatives gained extra leather trim on their instrument panels, together with an armrest. The Elegance and Avantgarde derivatives took on chromed tailpipes, and cruise control became optional right across the range.

2001: Mid-Life Facelift

Emissions concerns were also partly responsible for changes to the diesel models in February 2001. The A160 CDI was fitted with an intercooler to reduce emissions; one side benefit was that its engine now delivered 75PS instead of the original 60PS. The additional torque now made automatic transmission a viable option, and it became available for the A160 CDI at the same time. To maintain the differential between these models and the A170 CDI, the senior model was upgraded from 90PS to 95PS at the same time.

These changes were just part of a much more far-reaching overhaul of the A class range. In line with Mercedes' well-established policy, it had to be refreshed at or around the mid-point of its production life, and Stuttgart's engineers had been working on revisions for some time. In fact, the range overhaul occurred just three and a half years after the range's 1997 introduction, and just three years after its re-launch in February 1998 in re-worked form. It was slightly early for the half-way point in the model's production, which would not end until 2005.

Two things happened: the A class was given a facelift and the range was extended with the introduction of long-wheelbase models. In view of Mercedes' efforts to make the A class a small car, this was perhaps a surprising development – and all the more so because there was never any real shortage of legroom for rear-seat passengers in the original models. Nevertheless, the company bowed to demand. The long-wheelbase models, available with all the existing engine and gearbox combinations except the A160 CDI, had an extra 170mm (just under 7in) inserted into the wheelbase behind the centre door pillar. It increased overall interior space by 11 per cent and, according to Stuttgart, gave the long-wheelbase A class more rear legroom than a standard-wheelbase S class saloon!

The change entailed a redesign of the rear doors, which was done so skilfully that the extra length was not immediately obvious. In fact, it is arguable that the extra length made the car look better balanced, and there is no doubt that the longer wheelbase improved ride comfort. Load space was also increased, going up to a maximum of 1930 litres (68cu ft) – an impressive figure that was not far short of the 1975 litres (70cu ft) of the W210 E class estates. Brakes were revised to handle the extra weight, and the existing rear drums were

LEFT: *Another low-angle shot shows this 2001 standard-wheelbase car at its best.*

BELOW: *A low angle again! By the time this 2001 long-wheelbase model was pictured, the Mercedes press photographers had clearly worked out how to show the car to best advantage.*

The long-wheelbase models followed the styling lines established for the original short-wheelbase cars, as this picture comparing the two illustrates. All the extra length went into the rear doors.

matched by ventilated discs at the front, although the standard 15-in wheel size was retained. The extra cost of the long-wheelbase models, which were identified by an L after their designation, must have been a deterrent, but the cars became strong sellers nonetheless.

All the elements of the facelift were incorporated in the long-wheelbase models from the start of their production. This had been much more far-reaching than a casual glance would suggest, and had focused on revised front and rear-end details. At the front, changes had also improved the cars' aerodynamics to a small extent, so giving the potential for better fuel economy at speed.

Probably the most obvious change at the front was from the old three-slat grille to a four-slat type. This was finished in black on Classic models, in the body colour on Elegance derivatives, and in silver for the Avantgarde option. There were also clear glass headlamp covers, and alterations to the shape of the air intakes in the front apron. Protective rubber strips were also added to the corners of the car. These were finished in dark grey on Classic derivatives, while Elegance and

Avantgarde models had them in the body colour and topped by a bright metal trim strip.

These protective strips were matched by similar items at the rear, and the cumulative effect of these changes was to make the A class some 31mm (just over an inch) longer overall. The tail-light lenses changed, too, following the fashion for bichromatic types: instead of red, clear and amber lenses in the cluster, the new lenses were red and clear (on Classic and Elegance models) or red and smoked grey (on the Avantgarde models). The release button for the tailgate was changed, too, for a more practical handle with a recessed finger-grip.

While Classic models retained black door handles, Elegance and Avantgarde types had bright inserts added to their body-coloured handles. Inevitably, there were new wheel styles as well, the Classic gaining new ten-hole covers for its steel wheels, the Elegance moving to ten-hole alloys, and the Avantgarde taking on five-spoke alloys. Inside the cabin, there was a re-shaped fascia made from softer plastic, which countered some of the cheap feel of the earlier A class models; there was revised switchgear, some of it relocated; and there was

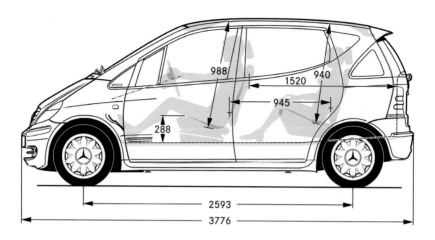

*Even the standard interior of an A class allowed a six-footer to sit comfortably behind a six-foot driver.
In the long-wheelbase models, legroom reached almost limousine-like levels.*

a new-look steering wheel on a column which now featured mechanical height adjustment. To the existing front and rear airbags was added the option of side 'curtain' airbags.

Stuttgart also took the opportunity to upgrade specifications in a few cases. The CDI models were fitted with electric auxiliary heaters for the passenger compartment, as customers had complained that their engines took too long to transfer their heat to the cabin. The A140 now took on ventilated front disc brakes, and the A160 and A170 CDI gained solid rear discs in place of drums. This left the A160 CDI as the only model with the

ABOVE: *The long-wheelbase models were better proportioned than the original short-wheelbase cars, at least when seen from the side. This is an A170 variant.*

RIGHT: *Just as on bigger Mercedes, leather upholstery was available. This is a 2001 model: note the different ICE head system on this higher trim level.*

BELOW: *This long-wheelbase A190 has parking sensors neatly integrated into the rear bumper.*

Wood trim undoubtedly helped to give the A class interior some of the ambience of the bigger Mercedes models. This is a 2001 model. The integrated telephone system would have been an expensive extra-cost option.

original combination of solid discs at the front and drums at the rear. There were also minor improvements to the suspension across the range, which resulted in noticeably better ride and handling.

In the UK, the last few months of 2001 also saw the introduction of two limited-edition A class models as a boost to sales. September brought 250 examples painted in unmissable Canyon Orange; based on the A140 and A160 models, they also had 16in alloy wheels and air conditioning in place of the standard sunroof. The second limited edition followed in November and consisted of 1000 cars based on

---

How Fast? How Thirsty?

These figures are typical for A class cars, but variations in the car's equipment levels and load, and variations in driving style will cause differences that may be significant.

	0–60mph	*Max speed*	*Mpg (overall)*
A140	12.9secs	168km/h (105mph)	40 (7ltr/100km)
A140 auto	14.6secs	165km/h (103mph)	37 (7.6ltr/100km)
A160	10.8secs	181km/h (113mph)	39 (7.25ltr/100km)
A160 CDI	17.6secs	152km/h (95mph)	59 (4.75ltr/100km)
A170 CDI (90PS)	12.5secs	173km/h (108mph)	58 (4.85ltr/100km)
A170 CDI (95PS)	12.0secs	179km/h (112mph)	58 (4.85ltr/100km)
A170 CDI L	12.1secs	178km/h (111mph)	58 (4.85ltr/100km)
A190	8.8secs	197km/h (123mph)	36 (7.85ltr/100km)
A210 Evolution	8.2secs	202km/h (126mph)	36 (7.85ltr/100km)
A210 Evo auto	9.0secs	197km/h (123mph)	34 (8.3ltr/100km)

the A140 Classic in standard- or long-wheel-base form but equipped additionally with air conditioning, a ten-CD autochanger and 15-in alloy wheels.

2002: The A210 Evolution

There was still more development life in the M166 engine, and in early 2002 Mercedes announced a new top model for the A class range. Unashamedly aimed at performance enthusiasts, the A210 Evolution had a long-stroke version of the A190's engine, with a swept volume of 2084cc and a power output of no less than 140PS. Fitted with the five-speed 'sports' manual gearbox and the taller 3.72:1 final drive first seen on the A190, the car was capable of 201km/h (126mph) and would reach 60mph from standstill in 8.2 seconds – a positively indecent performance from something that had started life as an economical city car. It even sounded good under acceleration, which was not something that could be said of most other four-cylinder Mercedes engines of the time – and certainly not of the other A class models.

The A210 was the car that had originally been mooted as an AMG-badged model, but the AMG body kit fitted as standard was per-

Best Buys

Various factors can influence purchase costs from time to time, and it is not possible to take these into account here. However, in terms of practicality and enjoyment, these are the best A class models to buy.

If fuel economy is one of your priorities, go for an A140 with manual transmission or an A160 with manual transmission, in each case in the lighter, standard-wheelbase configuration.

For extra load-carrying space, the long-wheelbase models are the sensible option. The bigger the engine, of course, the more expensive it will be to run.

For maximum driving enjoyment, an A190 or A210 Evolution in short-wheelbase form has to be the choice. But these cars are not as cheap to run as the smaller-engined models; perhaps a C class might be a more sensible choice.

haps the only legacy of its AMG heritage. One way or another, it would always be a relatively low-volume model that was not sold in all the A class markets. Sales of around 100 examples a month world-wide ensured it would retain its exclusivity to the end.

That bigger engine was not the only

AMG did not want to put their name on the A210 because they could not make it go fast enough, but the A210 Evolution (to use its full title) was nevertheless a respectably quick car.

123

Performance models demand a body kit to make them look faster as well as go faster. This is an A190 on the standard wheelbase.

mechanical change. The A210 had stiffer springs and dampers, although its ride height remained unchanged, and the ESP system had been recalibrated to suit. The brakes were the same ventilated front discs and solid rear discs as on the A190 and, like the A190, the A210 had a drive-by-wire accelerator. Available in both standard- and long-wheelbase forms, the A210 could even be had with automatic transmission, which took some of the sporting edge off its performance and also made it the thirstiest-ever variant of the A class.

The A210 also had some other special exterior features, notably a special silver-painted grille with three 'drilled' slats, and black polycarbonate aerodynamic fairings glued to either side of the tailgate. A red coachline along the body sides was part of the standard specification, but this could be deleted at no extra cost. Further recognition features came in the shape of the twin-oval chromed tailpipe and small oval 'Evolution' badges over the holes in the front wings that had carried side repeater indicators on earlier models. The indicators were moved to the door mirrors. The interior was specially equipped, too, featuring leather and alcantara trim, aluminium dash panels and a white-faced speedometer.

The rest of the A class range continued largely unchanged for the next three years, although in the UK there was a change in the model mix in March 2003 when the A160 CDI, previously unavailable in that market, was introduced.

Epilogue

The final W168 A class cars came off the assembly lines in Rastatt in 2005, 12 years after the Vision A Concept had been presented at the Frankfurt Motor Show, and just over seven years after production had begun in earnest after that near-disastrous false start.

Some 1.1 million cars of all types had been built. It was a convincing start for a model that was wholly new to the Mercedes brand and took it into a market sector where it had never been represented before. The A class had also formed the basis of another model for Mercedes – the 414-series Vaneo – which was introduced in 2001 as a compact MPV. The Vaneo was not a big success, partly perhaps because of its high price when compared to comparable vehicles from Renault or Opel/Vauxhall, but also undoubtedly because of its somewhat ungainly styling. However, it did form a sound basis for future model development, as indeed the A class had done. Mercedes had enough faith in its smallest model to replace the W168 in 2005 with a second-generation A class, a much more resolved design which promised even greater things.

Specifications for W168 A Class Models

Engines

Petrol estates

A140	1397cc M166 4-cyl, 82PS & 130Nm	(1997–2005)
A140 automatic	1598cc M166 4-cyl, 82PS & 140Nm	(2000–2005)
A140 L	1397cc M166 4-cyl, 82PS & 130Nm	(2001–2005)
A140 L automatic	1598cc M166 4-cyl, 82PS & 140Nm	(2001–2005)
A160	1598cc M166 4-cyl, 102PS & 150Nm	(1997–2005)
A160 L	1598cc M166 4-cyl, 102PS & 150Nm	(2001–2005)
A190	1898cc M166 4-cyl, 125PS & 180Nm	(1999–2005)
A190 L	1898cc M166 4-cyl, 125PS & 180Nm	(2001–2005)
A210 Evolution	2084cc M166 4-cyl, 140PS & 205Nm	(2001–2005)
A210 Evolution (LWB)	2084cc M166 4-cyl, 140PS & 205Nm	(2001–2005)

Diesel models

A160 CDI	1689cc OM668 4-cyl, 60PS & 160Nm	(1998–2001)
	1689cc OM668 4-cyl, 75PS & 160Nm	(2001–2005)
A170 CDI	1689cc OM668 4-cyl, 90PS & 180Nm	(1998–2001)
	1689cc OM668 4-cyl, 95PS & 180Nm	(2001–2005)
A170 CDI L	1689cc OM668 4-cyl, 95PS & 180Nm	(2001–2005)

Transmissions

Five-speed manual
Five-speed manual with Automatic Clutch System
Five-speed automatic

Running gear

Front suspension with wishbones, McPherson struts, twin-tube gas dampers and anti-roll bar.
Rear suspension with trailing arms, coil springs, single-tube gas dampers and anti-roll bar.

Dimensions

Wheelbase:	2423mm (95in) (standard-wheelbase models) or 2593mm (102in) (long-wheelbase models)
Front track:	1523mm (60in)
Rear track:	1472mm (58in)
Length:	3575mm (141in) (standard-wheelbase models to 2001); 3606mm (142in) (standard-wheelbase models from 2001); 3776mm (149in) (long-wheelbase models)

Width:	1719mm (68in)
Height:	1575–1589mm (62–62.5in), depending on wheel and tyre choice

Weights (typical)

A140 to Feb 1998:	1085kg (2387lb)
A140 from Feb 1998 and A160 to Feb 1998:	1095kg (2409lb)
A160 from Feb 1998:	1115kg (2453lb)
A140 L:	1135kg (2497lb)
A160 CDI:	1145kg (2519lb)
A190 and A210:	1155kg (2541lb)
A170 CDI:	1175kg (2585lb)
A170 CDI L:	1190kg (2618lb)

8 Junior SLs

The SLK Roadsters, 1996–2004

By the end of the 1970s, the US sports-car market was in turmoil; what had once been the world's largest market for such machines had dwindled to practically nothing. There were three main reasons for this: first, emissions control legislation had forced car makers to add performance-sapping weight to their cars; second, increasing oil prices had made 'fun' cars seem socially unacceptable; and third, car makers generally had been seriously scared by the possibility that open cars would be banned on safety grounds.

Mercedes-Benz soldiered on with its SL models, secure in the knowledge that they were the safest open sports cars on the market and confident that technology then under development would allow future models to circumvent a legislative ban. (In fact, there

The first SLKs were characterized by black sills and chin spoiler, and by a front apron with a horizontal bar. The bright yellow paint of this car, an SLK 230 Kompressor, was typical of the colours ordered in the late 1990s before silver became the top choice.

The black lower section extended right around the car on early models. The general shapes of the tail lights and the boot lid followed current Mercedes practice, but there was something almost cheeky about their execution on the SLK.

never would be any ban on open cars, either in America or anywhere else.) As for extra weight, engine development would take care of that; and the typical SL buyer was largely unconcerned by what the general public thought of his or her 'fun' car.

It was the market for much cheaper open sports cars that was hardest hit. The British manufacturers that had traditionally led the market did not replace their older designs when these reached the end of their production life; the Italians did much the same; and American domestic manufacturers ensured that any new sports cars they introduced had fixed roofs. During the 1980s, open sports cars almost ceased to exist.

However, many manufacturers were beginning to look at building traditional roadsters once again, as the threat of legislation to outlaw them receded. By the end of the decade, Stuttgart's product planners were looking at the possibility, and the tremendous success of Mazda's MX-5 roadster, introduced in 1989, proved that the market was ready for such a car. By 1991, the MX-5 was selling 70,000

units a year and had set an example no other manufacturer could afford to ignore.

A New Mercedes

In August 1992 the Mercedes-Benz Board met during an otherwise routine test session in Death Valley, California, and agreed that Stuttgart should build an 'affordable' roadster to meet this new demand. The agreement was subject to the car's ability to meet some defined cost and production targets, and it was already clear that this could only be achieved if it was based on the platform of the W202 saloon, the development of which was already well advanced.

Jorg Prigl was put in charge of project R170. He was asked to deliver a small roadster with a target weight of just 1200kg (2640lb), a youthful design and a collection of visible innovative technical features that would make it appeal to its intended young audience. Foremost among these was an innovative retractable steel hard top, which would replace the traditional folding soft top and removable

The black lower sections disappeared for 2001, giving way to body-coloured lower panels. It is interesting to compare the effect on this red car with the earlier red example on page 127.

hard top. There was a very tight dimensional package, and the design team were instructed to differentiate the new car very clearly from the existing SL so that it did not affect the established car's sales.

By the end of the year, their first thoughts had been translated into around a dozen one-fifth scale models. Some of these were deliberately 'retro' in style, harking back to earlier iconic Mercedes models such as the 190SL of the 1950s, the last 'junior SL' that the company had built. Others were more consciously modern, and it was one of these (designed by Michael Mauer) that was chosen for further development early in 1993. By May that year, still some three years away from production, the design was frozen.

Those three years would however not simply be used to develop the car to production readiness. It was equally important to prepare the buying public for the introduction of the new 'junior SL', and there is little doubt that

Stuttgart insisted on this because there were already clear signs that Alfa Romeo, BMW, Fiat and MG were already working on cars aimed at the same target buyers. Two fully functional 'concept cars' were built, to be displayed at motor shows. Both were very close to the eventual production car, but both had important (and deliberately misleading) differences from the chosen design.

The first one to break cover was a gold car, which starred on the Mercedes-Benz stand at the Turin Motor Show in April 1994. This car was fully driveable, and was in fact evaluated later by a number of magazines, including Britain's *Autocar*. Displayed as 'Studio SLK' (Italian for SLK Concept), it showed that the car would be a strict two-seater with an upswept waistline, sharply cut-off tail and a very distinctive Mercedes character. However, designer Peter Arcadipane had made it subtly different from the production design by lowering the winsdscreen, removing the rubber bumper inserts and changing the lights and grille.

The twin 'racing' fairings Arcadipane had added behind the headrests were perhaps pure show car, and so was the interior, with its red leather, silver and grey detailing and carbon-fibre trim. No one who saw the car can seriously have thought that it would go into production without any roof at all, even though the show car had none, and industry watchers no doubt suspected that the production model would have something other than the 150bhp current-production 2.2-litre four-cylinder engine under its steeply raked bonnet. However, the car on display looked fabulous, and that was what mattered.

The second car appeared at the Paris Motor Show that October, and deliberately displayed a different aspect of the R170's character. This time, the clever folding hard top was fitted, but the car was painted blue with matching blue wheels to give an impression of high performance, which contrasted with the cheeky,

fashionable appeal of the Turin prototype. 'Etude SLK' (French for 'SLK Concept') was very well received, and Mercedes knew they were on the right track. The 'K' in the title, by the way, probably stood for *kurz* (German for 'short') or *klein* ('small').

The public relations people rather incautiously admitted that the appearance of these two concept cars was intended to generate 40,000 advance orders – which would represent two years' production at the Bremen plant, where the car was to be built alongside the existing SL. In the event, only 25,000 firm orders had been taken by the time the new car went on sale, in mid-1996, but that was a figure of which any manufacturer would have been enormously proud.

1996: Enter the SLK

Three versions of the SLK were announced in the beginning. The entry-level car was the SLK200, powered by the latest 136bhp version

The SLK could be transformed from open roadster to snug fixed-roof coupé in a remarkably short space of time, which made it a practical roadster even in countries like the UK, where days like the one on which this picture was taken are few and far between.

of Mercedes' 2-litre four-cylinder engine with variable valve timing. This came with a five-speed manual gearbox as standard, when it took 9.5 seconds to reach 60mph from rest, or with a five-speed automatic at extra cost, when it needed 10.1 seconds to reach that speed. Maximum with either transmission was 206km/h (129mph). These were respectable figures, but Stuttgart considered the car was not fast enough to meet expectations in some markets and so it was not put on sale everywhere. Britain was one of the key markets which never received the model.

Not every market received the second model, either. This had a supercharged version of the 2-litre engine and was known as the SLK200 Kompressor. With 192bhp, it was only a touch less powerful than the third model, the bigger-engined SLK 230 Kompressor, but it was less accelerative because of the engine's lower torque. This car was sold in markets – Croatia, Greece, Italy and Portugal – where engine size was an important factor in avoiding extra taxation. It was another model that did not (at least at this stage) reach Britain.

The third model – which did reach Britain, in January 1997 – was the SLK230 Kompressor, which featured the new 193bhp supercharged 2.3-litre four-valve engine. With this engine, the automatic option delivered quicker acceleration to 100km/h (7.5 seconds as opposed to 7.6 seconds for the manual car), while the top speed of 227km/h (142mph) was just a whisker behind the manual's 230km/h (143mph). Some countries, Britain included, took only the automatic. Sadly, however, the supercharged engine sounded no more exciting in the SLK than it had in the W202 saloons released in the autumn of 1995; Stuttgart never did manage to do anything about this.

It was probably weight that had made the SLK200 disappointingly slow. Despite the use of magnesium in some areas of the monocoque, the production cars weighed in at 1270kg (2794lb) (1325kg/2915lb for the SLK230 Kompressor), which was rather more than the 1200kg target the designers had set. The SLK shape did incorporate several aerodynamic touches: a small lip on the boot lid

The perforated grille was black on early cars, but changed to a silver-grey finish on later examples.

The clever Vario roof folded at the top of the rear screen. This picture shows the join at the top of the rear roof pillar.

reduced drag by around 1 per cent, and miniature spoilers ahead of the front wheels deflected air downwards to reduce front-end lift at speed. With the roof up, the result was a Cd of 0.33, which was good, although certainly not spectacular.

It was undoubtedly that remarkable folding roof that provided much of the SLK's appeal in the beginning. It fulfilled the original design brief that the car should incorporate visible high-technology, and it gave the SLK automatic status as a fashion icon. Yet observers with longer memories would have recognized that it was not a completely new concept: a cruder version of the same idea had been pioneered nearly forty years earlier on the 1957 Ford Skyliner in America.

The great thing about what Stuttgart called the Vario roof was the fact that it did away with the need for a folding soft top, which had always made cars vulnerable to theft and vandalism and also tended to deteriorate badly with time. It also avoided the need for a cumbersome and expensive hard top like the SL's, which had to be stored somewhere when it

was not in use. With the Vario roof up, the driver simply had to touch a button and the whole roof would fold backwards and away into the boot – the boot lid raised on hinges at the back automatically – in 25 seconds. Safety interlocks prevented this from being done while the car was moving, but it all happened fast enough to be done while waiting at traffic lights. With the roof neatly stowed in the boot, another touch on the same button would put the process into reverse, turning the open car into a closed one before a summer shower had really had time to dampen the occupants' enthusiasm.

There were some drawbacks, of course. Boot space was considerably reduced when the Vario roof was stowed and, if the boot had been filled with the roof up, it was important to redistribute the load before trying to put it down! However, the whole system had otherwise been thought out very carefully, and ingenious design allowed the boot lid to hinge at its forward edge for access to luggage even though it hinged the other way to accept or release the Vario roof.

Both of those first models came with the Vario roof as standard, and a comprehensive standard specification that also included alloy wheels, sports seats, a leather-bound steering wheel, pop-up rollover bars behind the seats, a mesh-type draught-stopper which could be stretched across them, and central locking. The SLK was the first Mercedes ever to be sold without a proper spare wheel: in some countries the car simply came with tyre sealant and an electric pump to deal with punctures, while in others (including the UK) it came with a 'space-saver' emergency spare tyre and wheel. Extra-cost options included air conditioning, cruise control, leather upholstery, side airbags, bigger wheels with wider rims at the rear, and the automatic transmission on the SLK230 Kompressor.

More expensive than the Mazda MX-5, comparable to the four-cylinder BMW Z3, but considerably cheaper than the Porsche Boxster, the SLK was an instant world-wide hit. Its cheeky appearance, sporty handling (despite recirculating-ball steering inherited from the W202 saloons) and on-board gadgetry attracted the younger customers whom Mercedes had been targeting. Its price also attracted not a few older customers, who saw it as a sound investment for a second car or a retirement toy. For four full years – until the mid-point of the SLK's planned production life – Stuttgart found no reason to make major alterations to the SLK formula.

2000: Mid-Life Makeover

The mid-point of the SLK's planned production life was deemed to be February 2000, when Mercedes embarked on a complete overhaul of the range. Not only was there a facelift to freshen the cars' appearance, but there were also new models to broaden the SLKs' appeal. The old SLK200 was replaced in all markets by an SLK200 Kompressor, much improved from the earlier export model of the same name. The SLK230 Kompressor remained at the heart of the range, improved

in some areas, and a new six-cylinder car called the SLK320 was introduced to take the range upwards into new market territory. A significant improvement was the introduction across the range of a six-speed manual gearbox, the SG-S 270, to replace the earlier five-speed type. The five-speed automatic remained the alternative.

The front-end facelift brought silver-grey grille slats in place of the earlier black ones, retractable headlamp wash-wipes, and new fog lamps like those on the recently announced C215 coupés. Xenon headlamps were a new option. The rubber bump-strips in the apron were also divided into sections, to make replacement cheaper; this modification was also seen at the rear of the car. The rear light clusters took on the expected bi-chromatic lenses, there was a new boot release that made one-handed operation feasible, and the exhaust tips were finished in bright stainless steel.

Door handles and sills were now finished in the body colour, and a range of new alloy wheels was introduced. The 2-litre car had the same seven-hole wheels as the SLK200 it replaced, but there were new six-spokes for the SLK230 Kompressor, and new five-spokes for the SLK320. All models gained turn indicator repeaters in the door mirror housings.

Entering the car, new sill tread-plates were the first thing to catch a user's eye. These now carried the letters 'SLK' or, on SLK320 models, the 'V6' legend. The seats now had stronger side bolsters, and there was an electric adjustment option. There was a new four-spoke steering wheel, which could be replaced at extra cost by a smart item with a wood and leather rim. A turned metal finish for the centre console inlay replaced the earlier carbon-fibre type, and on the dash were additional lights for the ASSYST service interval indicator and for the EOBD emissions equipment monitoring system.

Last but not least, there were also invisible changes to the cars. The bonnet had been stiffened to improve ridigity, the fuel tank had been enlarged from 53 litres (11.5 gallons) to 60 litres (13 gallons), and the wind deflector had been slightly modified. ESP, BAS, and Speedtronic cruise control were now standard across the range.

The biggest news, though, was the arrival of that six-cylinder model. Mercedes had earlier denied that a six-cylinder SLK was planned, but many industry watchers found this hard to believe, and BMW's introduction of a six-cylinder Z3 for 1997 led many commentators to suggest that Mercedes would have to follow suit. Perhaps it was true that no six-cylinder SLK had been planned in the beginning, but the compact dimensions of Stuttgart's acclaimed new V6s made it relatively easy to drop one of these engines into the space designed to accommodate a four-cylinder when the SLK had its mid-life makeover in the summer of 2000.

The choice of engine was pretty well automatic, and few people can have been surprised to see that the new SLK320 had the 3.2-litre M112 V6 engine under its bonnet. Where the four-cylinder cars had been criticized for having only adequate performance, the new 218 PS engine turned the SLK into an altogether more sporting machine, with a 0–60mph time of 7.1 seconds and a maximum speed of 235km/h (147mph). It was, of course, considerably more expensive than the four-cylinder models and, as might have been expected, it came only with automatic transmission in some markets. For some tastes, it looked too much like the lesser SLKs, though. Only the rear badging, the wheels, and a front air intake with two vertical divisions differentiated it from the four-cylinder cars.

2001: The AMG SLK

The SLK320 was only the start of it. For those who wanted (and could afford) even more performance, Mercedes was already planning a new top-model SLK with a supercharged version of the V6 engine. Developed in conjunction with its AMG partner, and badged as an SLK32 AMG, this new model reached its first

The AMG model had a unique front apron and AMG's own wheels to distinguish it from lesser models. The 'V6 Kompressor' badge is just visible on the front wing.

ABOVE: *The heart of any AMG model is always its engine, and this is the AMG-modified 3.2-litre V6 of an SLK32 AMG. Also visible are the special wheels with their AMG logos.*

LEFT: *Twin tailpipes and that logo… it can only be the high-performance derivative of the SLK.*

*As always, AMG came up
with a special interior
treatment for their high-
performance model.
Note in particular the
instrument dials, and the
AMG logo on the kick-
plates and seat backrests.*

customers in January 2001. However, it would always be built in limited volumes, and only 4333 were made in just under three years of production. Just over 2000 of these were sold in the USA, while Germany had fewer than 1000 and the UK took fewer than 300.

As always with an AMG product, the key to the new SLK lay in its engine. Although this was based on the M112 V6 and retained its

3.2-litre swept volume, it had been extensively re-worked. AMG had added a Lysholm-type (twin-screw) supercharger made by IHI, and provided it with its own intercooler. In order to withstand the extra strains that this would impose on the engine, there had been major changes to the internal components. These included a stronger crankshaft, new pistons, camshafts that gave a longer overlap, a higher

LEFT, OPPOSITE AND BELOW: This selection of shots showing a late right-hand-drive SLK32 AMG was taken by UK enthusiast Tim Imrie. By this stage (as Tim apologetically admits), the combination of silver bodywork with black seats was becoming more or less standard!

This SLK is wearing AMG wheels and an AMG body kit: note the shapes of the sills and the front apron.

oil flow rate and of course a completely re-mapped ECU. The results were a power output of 354PS at 6100rpm, with maximum torque of 450Nm at 4400rpm.

It was mildly surprising to find that AMG had chosen not to mate this new powerhouse of an engine to the latest six-speed Mercedes gearbox. Instead, the SLK32 AMG was available only with a five-speed automatic transmission. However, this had been over-hauled to provide finger-tip shifting, lock-up in all gears, an automatic downshift to give engine braking under hard deceleration, and an automatic gear hold which operated in

Mercedes never believed in hiding their light under a bushel, even though they did believe in the value of discretion. All the supercharged SLKs had one of these badges on each front wing.

hard cornering. It certainly left nothing to complain about: the SLK32 AMG would reach 60mph from a standing start in 5.2 seconds, and in its time was the fastest-accelerating Mercedes-Benz car ever built (honourable exception being made, of course, for the hugely expensive C199 SLR McLaren, which would hit 60mph in 3.8 seconds). The car's top speed was restricted to 250km/h (155mph) under the 'gentlemen's agreement' that the leading German manufacturers still upheld – but for those who asked nicely, AMG were prepared to replace that speed limiter with one that restricted the maximum speed to 280km/h (174mph).

There were sufficient reserves in the car's re-worked underpinnings to cope with such a speed. AMG had fitted bigger brake discs all round, a stiffer rear anti-roll bar, and recalibrated springs and dampers. They had also

When not in use, the Vario roof folded away beneath a cover behind the seats. This view of a 2001 model shows the neat stowage arrangement, which did, of course, eat into what might otherwise have been luggage space in the boot.

gone for the long-established tuner's trick of fitting rear tyres that were wider than those at the front. In this case, the special double-spoke alloy wheels had 7.5in rims at the front and 8.5in rims at the rear, and these were shod respectively with 225/45 R 17 and 245/40 R 17 tyres. Even so, there were those who argued that the car's handling was not as crisp as it could have been at the limit.

Recognizing the AMG car was no problem, even from a distance. The wheels were an instant giveaway, but there were also a larger front air intake, twin oval tailpipes, and a dis-

creet boot-lid lip spoiler, which was claimed to increase downforce on the rear wheels by up to 50 per cent at high speeds. Closer to the car, 'V6 Kompressor' badges on each front wing confirmed that this was indeed the top model of the R170 range.

Owners were treated to some special interior features, too. The 300km/h (185mph) speedometer was perhaps a necessity, but there were pleasant touches in the sports seats with integral headrests, the two-tone leather upholstery, and the AMG steering wheel.

BELOW: *The standard interior was both sporty and welcoming. This is one of the colour options available in 2001, seen on an SLK320. The V6 emblem on the kick-plate was a neat touch.*

OPPOSITE: *This bright and contrasting choice of interior trim was seen on a 2001 SLK.*

Best Buys

Various factors can influence purchase costs from time to time, and it is not possible to take these into account here. However, in terms of practicality and enjoyment, these are the best R170 SLK models to buy.

The most popular SLK was always the SLK230 Kompressor, and deservedly so. Despite its singularly uninspiring exhaust note, it offers a good combination of affordable running costs and strong performance. Six-speed models are slightly quicker than the earlier five-speed types, and the automatics lose out mainly in heavier fuel consumption and maximum speed.

The SLK200 Kompressor does not lag far behind in performance, and is definitely worth a look. Least favourite is the early SLK200 with the naturally aspirated engine simply because it is quite a lot slower than the other models, especially in automatic form. However, if performance is not an important consideration, there is nothing to be said against an SLK200.

If performance matters a lot, then the SLK320 has to be the model to choose. It certainly is quick, has an enjoyably sporty exhaust note, and embodies everything that the SLK range was intended to be about. Fuel economy will be poorer than on four-cylinder cars, and running costs generally higher.

The SLK32 AMG is a wonderful car, but delivers more performance than most owners will ever need or be able to use. Its rarity and the AMG badge mean that it will always be expensive to buy relative to the other R170 SLK models, and of course running costs, insurance and fuel consumption will all count against it for the average owner. This is a car that is best left for the owner who can comfortably afford to run it, and as a dream for others.

ABOVE AND OPPOSITE: *Special editions found their way into the Mercedes marketing strategy as the new century opened. These pictures show the SLK Final Edition available in 2004. Note the special badge on the front wing.*

Epilogue

With these revisions, Mercedes seemed to have got the SLK range right on target once again. Sales remained strong until production ended in 2004, the last car being built at the Bremen plant on 7 April. It had been a sufficiently popular range to merit assembly overseas from CKD kits as well, and a number of SLKs had been assembled at the East London plant in South Africa.

Perhaps the clearest indication that Stuttgart had got the formula right was the fact that the replacement R171 range stuck very closely to the principles pioneered by the original SLK eight years earlier.

How Fast? How Thirsty?

These figures are typical for W170 SLK models, but variations in the car's equipment levels and load, and variations in driving style will cause differences that may be significant.

	0–60mph	Max speed	Mpg (overall)
SLK200 5-speed	9.3secs	206km/h (129mph)	31 (9ltr/100km)
SLK200 Kompressor	7.7secs	230km/h (143mph)	31 (9ltr/100km)
SLK230 Kompressor 6-spd	7.2secs	238km/h (149mph)	30 (9.4ltr/100km)
SLK230 Kompressor auto	7.3secs	226km/h (141mph)	29.5 (9.5ltr/100km)
SLK320	6.9secs	243km/h (152mph)	25.5 (11ltr/100km)
SLK320 auto	6.9secs	240km/h (150mph)	27 (10.5ltr/100km)
SLK32 AMG	5.2secs	250km/h (155mph) (limited)	25 (11.3ltr/100km)

Specifications for R170 SLK Models

Engines

SLK200	1998cc M111 4-cyl, 136PS & 190Nm	(1996–2000)
SLK200 Kompressor	1998cc M111 4-cyl, 192PS & 270Nm	(1996–2000)
	1998cc M111 4-cyl, 163PS & 230Nm	(2000–2004)
SLK230 Kompressor	2295cc M111 4-cyl, 193PS & 280Nm	(1996–2000)
	2295cc M111 4-cyl, 197PS & 280Nm	(2000–2004)
SLK320	3199cc M112 V6, 218PS & 310Nm	(2000–2004)
SLK32 AMG	3199cc M112 V6, 354PS & 450Nm	(2000–2004)

Transmissions

Five-speed manual (to 1999)
Six-speed manual (from 2000)
Five-speed automatic

Running gear

Front suspension with twin unequal-length wishbones, coil springs, gas dampers and anti-roll bar.
Rear suspension with five links, coil springs and gas dampers.
Power-assisted rack-and-pinion steering.
Four-wheel disc brakes, ventilated at the front on all models and at the rear on SLK320 and SLK32 AMG; three-channel ABS standard, with servo assistance. Tyres 205/60 R15 all round (SLK200); or 205/55 R16 front with 225/50 R16 at the rear; or 225/45 ZR 17 front with 245/40 ZR 17 rear.

Dimensions

Overall length:	3995mm (157in) (to 1999); 4010mm (158in) (from 2000)
Wheelbase:	2400mm (94in)
Overall width:	1715mm (67.5in)
Overall height:	1269–1284mm (50–50.5in), depending on tyre choice
Track:	1488mm (58.5in) (front); 1471–1485mm (58–58.5in) (rear, depending on tyre choice)

Weights (typical)

SLK200 Kompressor:	1325kg (2915lb) (to 1999); 1365kg (3003lb) (from 2000)
SLK320:	1405kg (3091lb)
SLK32 AMG:	1495kg (3289lb)

9   Coupés and Cabriolets

The 208-Series Cars

As early as 1987, when the coupé models of the 124-series were introduced, Mercedes-Benz had been quite clear about the future of its much-loved mid-sized two-door models. The 124s were to be the last of their kind, and in the future their replacements would not be derivatives of the marque's mid-range saloons. However, although Stuttgart was quite happy to make this much of its future intentions clear, it was not then prepared to explain that

its engineers were planning to build the next generation of coupés on the basis of the car which would replace the then-current W201 or '190' range.

The company's real intention was not made any clearer at the Geneva Motor Show in 1993, when it displayed a striking concept car that gave a good idea of the model that would replace the 124 coupés. The new model was still four years away from production, and the W202 C class that would replace the W201s and provide the platform for the new coupés

LEFT: That curved centre console helped to make the interior of the car feel more sporty. The trim option on this 2001 car shows that Mercedes had still not quite got over their attempt to brighten interiors with vivid patterns.

OPPOSITE, TOP: The media were still content with black and white pictures when the W208s were new, and this one shows an early CLK230 Kompressor with optional bright-finish wheels.

OPPOSITE, BOTTOM: The CLK's lines were well balanced, and the rear view was almost as attractive as the view from the front.

*The rising window-line gave the car a more sporty stance than its predecessors – the W124 coupés –
had enjoyed. This is a later car with turn signal repeaters mounted in the door mirror casings.*

was also several months away from going on
sale. So the Mercedes Concept Coupé had
been built on the platform and running gear
of the then-current W124 500E.

Nevertheless, hindsight shows that the car
was visually very close to the real thing. Styled
by Mercedes' Murat Günak and assembled by
ItalDesign, the concept car previewed the
twin-oval-headlamp styling which would
become a Mercedes hallmark much later in
the decade. Its curvaceous lines were unmistakeably those of the production W208 models, and its similarly curvaceous dashboard gave
a similarly clear preview of what was to come.
Only the drop-glasses in the rear body sides
and the panoramic perpsex roof would not
make it into the production cars, the drop-

glasses because of a need for extra body rigidity and the panoramic roof because that was
being held over until later for other models.

Radically new though it seemed at the
time, the concept coupé was very clearly a
member of the Mercedes-Benz family. Yet it
was an important step in the re-invention of
the Mercedes brand during the 1990s, and the
production car which came from it in June
1997 was vitally important in attracting new
customers to the marque. Some 40 per cent of
W208 customers were new to Mercedes, and
most of those were younger than the marque's
traditional buyers. So not only did the W208
replace the 124-series mid-range coupés, but it
was also a big success in attracting new business, some of which no doubt came from the

3-series coupés which had been such a big hit for BMW. In less than five years, Stuttgart sold 230,000 of the 208-series cars, including the cabriolet derivatives which appeared in 1999 and replaced – after an agonizing wait for some customers – the 124-series cabriolets.

Design

Using the W202 platform meant that the CLK (as the new model was known) sat on the same 2690mm (106in) wheelbase and featured the same double-wishbone front and multi-link rear suspension. However, it did benefit from the improvements made to the C class for the 1998 model-year, so the front suspension boasted longer spring travel, a wider track, a fatter anti-roll bar, twin hydraulic mounts and more compliant gas dampers than in the original C class.

Yet the CLK was 80mm (just over 3in) longer than a C class and, model for model, some 10kg (22lb) heavier. Unfortunately, it retained the power-assisted recirculating-ball steering of the C class, which was

well weighted but too slow in operation to match the sporting demeanour of the CLK. On the positive side, however, it did boast a well-balanced 'chassis' and excellent high-speed stability.

Inside, the seats had a new design, with lower cushions than in the C class, to compensate for the reduced headroom. Measurements showed that the CLK's interior space was actually greater than that of the cars it replaced, but it certainly did not feel that way: the thick rear pillars tended to make the rear seats feel more hemmed in, and the fixed B-pillar and side glasses contributed more to that impression. From the outside, though, it all looked different. Black-out glass concealed the B-pillar between waist and roof to make the car look as if it was a pillarless hard top like the old 124-series models.

There was no denying that the new CLK was an extremely attractive design. The overall effect of its upswept waistline and those thick rear pillars was to suggest a cat poised and ready to strike. The car almost looked as if it was moving even when it was standing still.

This characteristically neat under-bonnet view shows the supercharged 2-litre four-cylinder engine in a CLK200 Kompressor coupé.

It was sexy rather than svelte in the tradition of earlier Mercedes coupés, and there was a hint of aggression about its stance when viewed from the front. The car was 82mm (just over 3in) lower than a C class saloon, with a more steeply raked windscreen to suit. As for those twin headlights, which were actually smaller than those on the E class, to suit the CLK's smaller frontal area, and more steeply raked, they did an admirable job of persuading customers that this was not a C class in a party dress but rather a relative of the bigger and more expensive E class saloons.

Right from the start, the CLK was marketed with two different trim levels and appropriate front-wing badging to match. The slightly more expensive Elegance trim offered a fairly sober range of interior colours, complemented by traditional burr walnut on door trims, console and dash. The instruments had traditional black faces, and bright trim provided discreet visual relief throughout. By contrast, the Sport trim was designed to appeal to younger buyers. There was imitation carbon-fibre where the Elegance had burr walnut, the bright metal trim was banished, the instruments had white faces and there was a range of brighter interior colours.

Stiffer springs and dampers were a no-cost option, which allowed the Sport variants to live up better to their name, although at the expense to some extent of ride comfort. Sport and Elegance were further differentiated by distinctive styles of alloy wheel. Sport models had polished seven-spoke types while Elegance models had dished five-spokes. There were, though, two additional options: AMG five-spoke wheels with a variant of that company's traditional monoblock design, and Evo six-spoke alloys as well.

The entry-level car was the CLK200, but the CLK200 Kompressor with supercharged 2-litre engine was a better proposition for those who wanted a sports coupé.

No doubt about it, there has always been an element of glamour associated with an open Mercedes of any kind. This press picture from 2001 paired blonde driver with red car to good effect.

1997: The First Coupés

The initial W208 release in 1997 brought just three engine options, although Mercedes let it be known that a high-performance AMG model with V8 power was in the works for 1998. Those first three engines went into the CLK200, the CLK230 Kompressor, and the CLK320. Neither of the two four-cylinders was new to Mercedes: both the 136bhp 2-litre and the 190bhp supercharged 2.3-litre four-cylinders were already in use in the C class and the SLK. However, the 218bhp 3.2-litre V6 was a brand-new engine which would only later be seen in the SL and SLK roadsters, the E class and S class saloons, and the ML class SUV.

Among them, these three models hit most of the bases that CLK customers seemed to want. There were no diesels – and never would be in these first-generation CLKs – but the buying public was not yet ready for a sporting diesel. The two four-cylinder cars came with six-speed manual gearboxes as standard, while the V6 always had the five-speed automatic, which was an extra-cost option on the four-cylinder models. As always, exactly what was available depended on the requirements of individual markets: in the UK, for example, the six-speed manual could be ordered on the entry-level CLK200 but not on the CLK230 Kompressor.

While 206km/h (129mph) and 0–60mph in 10.5 seconds made the manual CLK200 a bit less than sporting by the standards of the day, and its four-cylinder engine had a rather uninspiring exhaust note, the CLK230 Kompressor was more like it. This model promised 234km/h (146mph) and 60mph in 8.2 seconds, and its exhaust made much more sporting noises. However, for both aural entertainment and refinement, the CLK320 was the hands-down winner its elevated price led customers to expect. Maximum speed was 238km/h (149mph) while 60mph came up in 7.1 seconds.

Equipment levels of course varied from model to model and from country to country, but all CLKs were saddled with Mercedes' foot-operated parking brake, which somehow seemed to detract from their sporting nature. All of them had a one-third-two-thirds split-folding rear seat backrest, which usefully increased the carrying capacity of the already large boot, and for those who really needed it there was an optional ski-bag. The front seats had a very effective pull-and-slide mechanism to make access to the rear seats easy. For extra cost, the front seats were all-electric, which meant power-assistance for the pull-and-slide mechanism and for the seat adjustment (complete with a position memory), plus heated cushions. Side airbags and seat-belt pre-tensioners were standard in most countries.

Turning the W208 into a cabriolet was always anticipated, but the car turned out to be rather more attractive and practical than many observers had expected. The model brought an open four-seater back into the Mercedes range after an absence that, for some, had been too long.

Speedmatic cruise control was available, as were the ASSYST service interval indicator and the ELCODE keyless start system, which consisted of a high-tech stub containing a microchip; it had to be inserted into a socket in the dash and then turned like a conventional key. The new Brake Assist system (which sensed a panic stop and automatically delivered full braking power), ASR traction control and electronic throttle control were all there, and ESP stability control could be had as an option on the CLK320 but not on the lesser models. Parktronic parking sensors, Xenon headlamps, rain-sensor wipers, leather upholstery, air conditioning, satellite navigation, self-levelling suspension and an electric glass sunroof were all on the options list. In adition, enthusiastic drivers could specify 8-in wheel rims at the rear shod with wider 225/50R16 tyres.

1998: Enter the Cabriolets...

Late in the life of the 124-series two-doors, Stuttgart had introduced cabriolet derivatives, which had immediately found an enthusiastic market. This was not a market to be lost, and cabriolet versions of the 208-series CLKs had been included in the design programme from the start. However, they were not released until a year after the coupé models, partly to simplify the early days of production but also to allow a healthy waiting list to build up.

The company need hardly have bothered about building up waiting lists. Even though the CLK cabriolets were announced at the Geneva Show in 1998, less than a year after the last of the 124-series E class cabriolets had been made, the waiting list had already reached truly epic proportions. Mercedes management hastily accepted that their sales forecasts had been way too pessimistic and increased the build capacity of the cabriolets from 18,000 to 23,000 a year. Even that was not enough, and by the time the CLK cabriolets reached the market in June 1998, they were already sold out until well into the next century.

There was no doubting that the CLK cabriolet had stunning visual appeal. The heavy haunches of the coupé were eliminated with the fixed roof, and a neat metal tonneau with small speedster-type humps over the hood well gave a very clean look to the rear of the car.

The later style of steering wheel is seen here on a right-hand-drive CLK430 cabriolet.

Boot space was compromised with the top down – it reduced from 350 litres (12cu ft) to 237 litres (8.5cu ft) – but probably few buyers cared. That triple-layer convertible top itself had a proper glass backlight, complete with heating element, and came in three different colours: blue, black or green. It was, of course, power-assisted. The electrics took around 30 seconds to do their job, dropping the windows when needed and automatically raising and lowering the tonneau cover. However, the top had to be pulled down manually for the last inch or so before it could be locked to the windscreen frame. For obvious reasons, the car also had to be stationary with its boot closed before the convertible top mechanism would operate.

Mostly, the cabriolet's interior echoed that of the coupé, but the presence of that convertible top had brought certain compromises. The rear seat cushions were actually 52mm (just over 2in) shorter than those in the fixed-roof car, and they were mounted higher and more upright. A wind deflector could be had for extra cost to reduce buffeting when the top was down, but when this was erected there was no room for rear-seat passengers at all.

Of course, the cabriolet was some 225kg (495lb) heavier than the coupé, thanks to copious reinforcement under the skin. A large stiffening brace ran right around the passenger compartment's floor pan, and this, together with further stiffening of the A-pillars, added the extra kilos. The cabriolet had in fact been developed in conjunction with Karmann, which also assembled the bodies for Mercedes-Benz, and was remarkably rigid although mid-corner bumps could cause a certain amount of scuttle shake, when the extra weight and ponderous steering combined to make the cars feel almost ponderous. Not suprisingly, it incorporated for rollover protection the pop-up rear headrests that had been pioneered on the R129 SLs some nine years earlier.

Cabriolets were made available with all three engine options, although as usual the model mix was tailored to suit individual ter-ritories. The CLK200 cabriolet, for example, was never available in the UK, where the cars were always marketed with a more upmarket image than this model suggested. The extra weight and slightly poorer aerodynamics meant that 0–60mph times were around a second slower than for equivalent coupés, while top speeds were some 2mph down all round.

...And the V8 Models

North America's long-standing love-affair with the V8 engine must have persuaded Stuttgart to announce the next new CLK at a motor show in the USA – the Detroit International Motor Show in January 1998. The V8-powered CLK430 was just a tease at this stage, however: in many markets, including the UK, the car would not go on sale until the autumn of the following year. By that stage, the cabriolets had also been announced and the CLK430 became available in that body style as well.

Of course, no one was in any doubt that the new coupés and cabriolets were destined to be fairly low-volume niche models. Not every CLK buyer was going to want the 250km/h (155mph) maximum speed (it was electronically limited, of course) and 6.3-second 0–60mph time that these cars offered, and nor could every CLK buyer afford such an expensive machine.

From the time of the CLK's launch a year earlier, Mercedes had made no secret of the fact that the V8 model would be badged as a CLK430 or that it would have the latest twin-spark, three-valve 4.3-litre V8 engine. This came in 275bhp guise, with very useable torque of 295lb ft all the way from 3000 to 4500rpm, and was mated to a five-speed automatic gearbox with Tip-shift manual over-ride control. There were of course fatter tyres to keep all this power and torque under control, and the CLK430 came with 7.5J rims in a 17in diameter and 225/45 tyres all round. It also had the stiffened suspension of the Sport models. The result was a car that delivered exceptionally good handling – although enthusiastic

The soft top of the cabriolet models fitted as neatly as anyone could wish for, and made the car as snug as a fixed-roof model. The coloured pictures show a late model CLK230 Kompressor, with turn indicator repeaters in the door mirror bodies; the black and white picture is of an early car.

Top of the 'everyday' CLK range was the V8-powered CLK430, seen here in right-hand-drive cabriolet form.

drivers bemoaned the obligatory fitment of ESP, ETS and all the other Mercedes aids to safer driving.

With this car, it looked as if the CLK range had been topped off, because it was already clear that the cabriolets were going to be replaced during 2002 and that a second-generation CLK was under development for release in the early years of the new century. But, as usual, Mercedes was planning a mid-life facelift. The story of the W208 models was not over yet.

1999: Mid-Life Facelift

The facelift came in September 1999. There was an expanded model range, too, including the first AMG model (the CLK55 AMG) and a V8 engine for the cabriolets in the shape of a CLK430 derivative. Other changes included the introduction of the Pre-Safe suite of electronic safety aids and the standardization of ESP across the CLK range.

Most noticeably, the 2000 model-year CLKs introduced in 1999 had body-coloured sills and bumper inserts in place of the earlier black ones, and indicator repeaters on the door mirrors like the latest S class. Interior changes included a Tip-shift control on automatics, a COMAND screen in the central control stack, a new instrument dial with a multi-function dot-matrix display, a digital display for the gear selection in the rev counter on automatic models, and a leather-rimmed multi-function steering wheel like the one in the latest E class. For extra cost, buyers could order a combined wood-and-leather rim for this wheel. Manual-transmission cars could now be had with the Speedtronic cruise control earlier seen on automatics, and for cabriolets there was a remote boot-lid release on the centre console.

The earlier Sport trim option disappeared to be replaced by an Avantgarde specification, which was overall rather closer to the existing Elegance trim. However, Sport models had blue-tinted glass (instead of green in the Elegance), seven-hole alloy wheels (instead of five-hole types), and body-coloured door handles with no chrome highlights. Inside they had no chrome at all, but black highlights instead; the wood trim was also different and Sport trim brought its own upholstery.

The CLK55 AMG

The first AMG derivative of the CLK range was announced in September 1999 as a coupé only – the story was that there was insufficient production capacity at Affalterbach for a cabriolet as well – although the open-top version of the car did become available by the end of the year. In fact, the CLK55 AMG was a car that had not originally been planned, but a one-off example had been assembled for use as a safety car at Formula 1 race events, and its exposure on television led to a clamour for replicas.

Best Buys

Various factors can influence purchase costs from time to time, and it is not possible to take these into account here. However, in terms of practicality and enjoyment, these are the best W208 models to buy.

Only 400 CLK55 AMG cabriolets were built, and demand is high, so other types are much more easily attainable! Cabriolets of all kinds are rarer than coupés, and it is worth remembering that the fixed rear side windows of the coupés mean that they do not offer the same option of near-open-air motoring that could be had from their W124 predecessors.

That said, the most numerous cars are the CLK320 six-cylinder and CLK230 Kompressor four-cylinder models. Not for nothing was the CLK320 always the best-selling W208, but of course these six-cylinder cars are inevitably more expensive to run than the fours. They also sound a lot nicer! All the sixes have automatic gearboxes, and, although that should definitely not be counted against them, there are some drivers who simply prefer a manual.

As a result, the AMG-developed 5.5-litre V8 was squeezed into the CLK's engine bay and the production car became a reality. With 347bhp it was by far the most powerful of the CLKs, and its 0–60mph time of 5.5 seconds made it the fastest of the AMG-engined Mercedes, too. All cars came with five-speed automatic transmissions and the stiffened sports suspension, and they also had bigger brakes with ventilated discs both front and rear. The AMG star-spoke alloy wheels also wore tyres that were unique in the CLK range – 225/45ZR17s at the front (on 7.5in rims) and 245/40ZR17s at the rear (on 8.5in rims).

While the CLK55 looked pretty much like any other CLK, it did have some distinguishing features. To the wide tyres, AMG wheels and CLK55 boot-lid badge, it added re-shaped side skirts, which were claimed to be more aerodynamic, and a new front apron. This had round driving lamps in place of the shaped driving lamps on other CLKs, and larger air-intake slots.

For a car that had never been intended to go into production, the AMG version of the CLK sold startingly well, too. No fewer than 3381 coupés found buyers, along with 400 cabriolets. Both Mercedes and AMG learned a lesson from that experience.

2000: More New Engines

Stuttgart was still not done with changes to the CLK range, and in spring 2000 there was a series of improvements for the four-cylinder models. Most important was the introduction of new engines from the latest W203 C class models. There were also interior improvements across the range, affecting such things as the operation options of the sunroof and electric windows, and 17in alloy wheels were introduced as a new option.

Mercedes also took the opportunity to realign its range slightly, and to simplify the W208 production lines. The CLK200 with its 136bhp naturally aspirated engine went out of production, as did the special 192bhp CLK200 Kompressor built for export to Greece, Italy and Portugal. In place of the latter – and now available for other markets as well, including the UK – came a 163bhp CLK200 Kompressor, which was offered in cabriolet as well as coupé form. The existing CLK230 was meanwhile upgraded with an extra 4bhp to 197bhp. New arrangements for the supercharger installation did away with the need for the earlier (and sometimes troublesome) electro-magnetic clutch.

With these new engines, all the four-cylinder cars took on the latest SG-S 400 six-speed

Sills, front apron and wheels mark this car out as a CLK55 AMG cabriolet, while the side marker lamp visible at the end of the front bumper makes clear that the car was destined for the USA.

How Fast? How Thirsty?

These figures are typical for W208 CLK models, but variations in the car's equipment levels and load, and variations in driving style will cause differences that may be significant.

	0–60mph	Max speed	Mpg (overall)
CLK200 Kompressor (163bhp)	9.1sec	221km/h (138mph)	28 (10ltr/100km)
CLK230 Kompressor	8.4sec	232km/h (145mph) (manual)	25 (11.3ltr/100km)
CLK320	7.4sec	238km/h (149mph)	25 (11.3ltr/100km)
CLK430	6.4sec	250km/h (155mph) (limited)	23 (12.3ltr/100km)
CLK55 AMG	5.4sec	250km/h (155mph) (limited)	21 (13.5ltr/100km)

Note: cabriolet models are heavier than their coupé equivalents and are likely to be slightly thirstier in most circumstances.

---

manual gearbox, which could be ordered optionally with the Sequentronic electronic sequential shift.

...And, Finally, the CLK GTR

In fact, the CLK GTR was not the final version of the CLK to be introduced, as it arrived in 1998. Nor was it really a proper CLK, as the car had originally been developed for touring-car races and had only an outline resemblance to the 208-series cars. It did use real CLK tail-light clusters, and there were several production parts inside the cabin, but this was a very special machine indeed.

The CLK GTR was built by AMG in Ludwigsburg, near Stuttgart, and was deliberately intended as a rich person's plaything. In fact, only serious millionaires could afford one – each of the twenty-five hand-built cars cost around £1.1 million. Built around a carbon-fibre monocoque supplied by Lola Composites, the CLK GTR had removable front and rear panels and scissor-type doors to its two-seater cockpit.

Power – all 612bhp of it – came from a mid-mounted 6.9-litre V12 engine developed by AMG from the 6-litre Mercedes V12. This engine was mounted directly to the carbon-fibre bulkhead behind the cockpit and drove the rear wheels through a four-plate carbon-fibre clutch and a six-speed Xtrac competition gearbox with paddle shifts (the original competition car had actually had a floor gearchange). Both front and rear suspension depended on double wishbones with horizontal spring-and-damper units, but the rear suspension was bolted directly to the load-bearing engine. Running on Bridgestone 345/35ZR18 tyres all round, the road-going car stood just 100mm (4in) off the ground, which represented a welcome increase on the somewhat impractical 40mm (1.5in) of the racing versions. The steering, of course, was a rack-and-pinion system needing just two turns lock-to-lock.

As for performance, the CLK GTR had as much of it as could be expected from a tamed racing car. It would hit 60mph from rest in 3.6 seconds and go on to a maximum of 318km/h (199mph). Acceleration was simply breathtaking at any speed – but so was the ride, even though the road cars' suspension embodied rubber bushes in place of the rigid joints of the racing cars!

Success?

This first CLK range was undoubtedly a success. Mercedes had achieved the delicate balancing act of retaining a significant percentage of those customers who had previously bought the two-doors of the W124 range, based on the E class, while at the same time broadening the appeal of the cars to attract new customers. In addition, taking customers away from BMW's 3 Series two-door coupés and cabriolets had of course always been a key aim.

The final W208s were built in the summer of 2002, and by that time Mercedes had already displayed their W209 successors at the Geneva Show. Well over 630,000 cars had been built, and the strongest seller throughout had been the CLK320.

Specifications for W208 Models

Engines

Coupé models

CLK200	1998cc M111 4-cyl, 136PS & 190Nm	(1997–2000)
CLK200 Kompressor	1998cc M111 4-cyl, 192PS & 270Nm	(1997–2000)
	1998cc M111 4-cyl, 163PS & 230Nm	(2000–2002)
CLK230 Kompressor	2295cc M111 4-cyl, 193PS & 280Nm	(1997–2000)
	2295cc M111 4-cyl, 197PS & 280Nm	(2000–2002)
CLK320	3199cc M112 V6, 218PS & 310Nm	(1997–2002)
CLK430	4266cc M113 V8, 279PS & 400Nm	(1998–2002)
CLK55 AMG	5439cc M113 V8, 347PS & 510Nm	(1999–2002)

Cabriolet models

CLK200	1998cc M111 4-cyl, 136PS & 190Nm	(1998–2000)
CLK200 Kompressor	1998cc M111 4-cyl, 192PS & 270Nm	(1998–2000)
	1998cc M111 4-cyl, 163PS & 230Nm	(2000–2002)
CLK230 Kompressor	2295cc M111 4-cyl, 193PS & 280Nm	(1998–2000)
	2295cc M111 4-cyl, 197PS & 280Nm	(2000–2002)
CLK320	3199cc M112 V6, 218PS & 310Nm	(1998–2002)
CLK430	4266cc M113 V8, 279PS & 400Nm	(1999–2002)
CLK55 AMG	5439cc M113 V8, 347PS & 510Nm	(1999–2002)

Transmissions

Five-speed manual standard on four-cylinder models before May 2000, and six-speed manual with optional Sequentronic shift standard thereafter. Five-speed automatic optional on four-cylinder cars and standard on six-cylinders and V8s.

Running gear

Front suspension with double wishbones, coil springs, telescopic dampers and anti-roll bar.
Multi-link rear suspension with coil springs, telescopic dampers and anti-roll bar.
Power-assisted recirculating-ball steering.
Power-assisted brakes with ABS as standard; ventilated discs at the front and solid discs at the rear.

Dimensions

Overall length:	4567mm (180in)
Wheelbase:	2690mm (106in)
Overall width:	1722mm (68in)
Overall height:	1345mm (53in) (coupé);
	1380mm (54in) (cabriolet)
Track:	1505mm (59in) (front);
	1474mm (58in) (rear)

Weights (typical)

CLK200 Kompressor coupé:	1840kg (4048lb)
CLK230 Kompressor coupé:	1870kg (4114lb)
CLK230 Kompressor cabriolet:	2030kg (4466lb)
CLK320 coupé:	1920kg (4224lb)
CLK320 cabriolet:	2070kg (4554lb)
CLK430 coupé:	1960kg (4312lb)
CLK55 AMG coupé:	1960kg (4312lb)

---

10 The M Class Sports Utility

One of the most striking characteristics of the world automotive scene in the 1980s was the dramatic increase in the sales of 4×4 leisure vehicles, or Sport Utility Vehicles as they came to be known in the USA. The Mercedes-Benz marque was ill equipped to compete in this arena: its G-Wagen 4×4 was too uncompromisingly utilitarian to have a widespread appeal and, despite attempts to 'civilize' it, the vehicle was not a true SUV.

By March 1992, the first studies were being made into the desirability of building a

Mercedes-Benz SUV. Just seven months later – in October – the Daimler-Benz Board approved the basic plan. This plan was heavily influenced by two factors: first, there was nowhere obvious in the existing Daimler-Benz plants where assembly lines for the new vehicle could be fitted in; and, second, the biggest (and fastest-growing) market for SUVs was the USA.

The Board did not take long to reach its next decision. On 5 April 1993, some 13 months after those first SUV studies had been made, Daimler-Benz announced that it would

Good on-road behaviour was an integral part of the Mercedes SUV concept, and the car had to be good because it was going to go head-to-head with the much-praised BMW X5.

be building a new assembly plant in the USA specifically for its forthcoming new SUV.

At this stage, the precise location of the new plant had not been finally chosen, and there was still feverish activity going on behind the scenes. No fewer than thirty US states had either expressed an interest or put forward a firm tender to get the new Mercedes-Benz factory, and a Daimler-Benz team led by Andreas Renschler was allocated to pick the most suitable site. Working very much in secret, their choice eventually fell upon Alabama, where a site at Vance, near Tuscaloosa, had been identified as ideal. It promised good transport links to sea ports as well as a viable supplier infrastructure, an eager workforce and a high degree of support from the state government.

The announcement that Alabama had been selected was made on 30 September 1993, and the first ground was broken for the new factory (which would cover one million square feet) on 4 May 1994 – still only 26 months after the first SUV studies had been made in Stuttgart. This factory was not to be a carbon copy of any German Daimler-Benz assembly plant; instead, it was to pioneer new ways of working, which the company saw as essential to its future. It would be based on the latest 'just-in-time' assembly methods, where expensive buffer zones of components were eliminated in favour of a reliance on suppliers to deliver components as they were needed on the lines. Not only would local suppliers have to meet these tight schedules; the parent company in Germany, which would be supplying the engines and primary gearboxes for the new vehicle, would also have to comply.

The ML's off-road ability was certainly not negligible, as this publicity picture of a later model was intended to demonstrate. However, it was never intended to be a heavy-duty off-roader: for that, Mercedes already had the G-class in production.

Meanwhile, Daimler-Benz had run a number of customer clinics in the USA in order to understand the good and bad points of existing SUVs. The decision was taken to target the $35,000 bracket, which meant that the new Mercedes would compete head-on with top models of the Ford Explorer and Jeep Grand Cherokee. Different versions would be developed to suit other markets, but the key target was always the heartland of the USA.

Under the works code W163 – which, curiously, had also been used earlier for a single-seat racing Mercedes – the design team now got busy on the new vehicle. Early proposals ranged from a straightforward makeover and 'softening' of the existing G-Wagen to quite radical ideas, but in due course the outlines of the new vehicle became clearer. Work began to focus on five basic proposals, three from the Mercedes design studios in Germany, and one each from the company's design studios in California and Japan. The idea was to draw on influences from major potential markets around the world, but in the end one of the German designs was chosen for production.

The final appearance of the W163 was settled in the early spring of 1994. It was a quite remarkable design as far as the SUV market was concerned. Most SUVs in the 1990s were square and boxy, but the Mercedes designers had given their SUV a more rakish profile, with a sloping bonnet and a pair of slanted front lamp units alongside the latest shallow Mercedes grille to aid the 'streamlined' look. The W163 also boasted a softer, more rounded shape than any other 4×4 of the time – although BMW's rival X5 was in fact being designed along the same lines at the time. A long wheelbase promised the best possible ride, while the 'wheel-at-each corner' layout also minimized front and rear overhangs, to improve off-road performance. The Mercedes SUV's drag coefficient of 0.39 was not spectacular, but it was good for a vehicle of its type.

However, there were unmistakeably chunky 4×4 styling cues, too, and the vehicle looked as if it sat higher off the ground than it really did.

Wishbones and coils made up the front suspension of the ML. It was a classic road-car layout, although it performed tolerably well in the rough as well.

A top-hinged rear hatch recalled car rather than 4×4 practice, but for those who wanted to emphasize the tough off-roader image the designers provided an optional external spare-wheel mounting. To some eyes, this quite massive structure looked a little excessive, but it was also the only way of getting a full-size spare wheel with the vehicle: as standard, a space-saver spare was carried internally.

The issue of the W163's basic construction was decided very early on. As this was Daimler-Benz's first foray into the SUV market, the company had to be in a position to make quite major changes very quickly and as cheaply as possible if its new vehicle did not hit the target straight from the off. A car-style monocoque was considered to be too inflexible if major changes were needed, and so separate-chassis construction was chosen. This implied greater weight than was desirable for the vehicle.

However, the engineering team under Dr Gerhard Fritz did not follow the traditional method of mounting an unstressed body shell on to a load-bearing chassis frame. Instead,

The dashboard was almost generic Mercedes in concept, and was designed to remind the car's occupants that all the quality they had come to expect of Mercedes-Benz was present in this one too. This is a 2001 AMG model.

they reasoned that they could save weight by making the body itself strong enough to take most of the torsional stresses – as it does in a monocoque. This in turn would mean that the chassis frame did not have to be as strong and heavy, and in fact the end result was that as much as 70 per cent of the overall torsional rigidity came from the body. It represented almost a complete reversal of the way things were on the old-style G-Wagen.

The construction of the new SUV was complicated even further. In order to reduce noise transmission and improve refinement, both front and rear suspensions were carried on their own sub-frames, which were fitted to the chassis frame – and of course made their own contribution to the overall torsional stiffness. The front suspension used a forged aluminium upper A-arm and a steel lower one, while for packaging reasons it proved necessary to use torsion bar springs rather than the coil springs that might have been expected. There were progressive-rate coil springs at the rear, though, where a similar twin-arm system was used. Here, however, both arms were made of aluminium to save weight.

The choice of engines was really determined by the Mercedes car division's overall engine strategy. Still in the development stages as the new SUV was being drawn up was the family of modular V6 and V8 engines that would power the company's larger vehicles. The planned 3.2-litre V6 was an obvious choice, as was the forthcoming 4.3-litre V8. Both of these would be ideal for the US market, but in other territories they would be less suitable. So outside the USA, there would be versions of the W163 powered by the existing 2.3-litre four-cylinder petrol engine and by the latest 2.7-litre five-cylinder diesel.

As for transmissions, it was clear that there would be no significant demand for a manual gearbox, and so the choice fell quite naturally upon Mercedes' latest five-speed automatic. (Nevertheless, the 2.3-litre four-cylinder model was made available with a manual gearbox.) Already boasting a fuel-saving torque-converter lock-up feature, which operated on third, fourth and fifth gears, the automatic was further modified to lock into first gear on receiving signals from sensors when the vehicle was negotiating steep descents (the W163 was, after all, supposed to be suitable for off-road use as well as every-day road use). However, a stab on the accelerator pedal would over-ride the system to enable upchanges as required.

A low range of gears for off-road driving was provided by a dual-range transfer gearbox, manufactured by Borg Warner in the USA. Low range was selected electronically and engaged by a driver-friendly push-button on the dashboard. The transfer gearbox also provided permanent four-wheel drive, through a centre differential. The drive was split equally between front and rear pairs of wheels, one propshaft running forwards from the transfer box to the front wheels and one running backwards to drive the rear pair, in traditional off-roader fashion.

Nevertheless, the W163 was never intended to be a heavy-duty off-roader. Instead, its four-wheel drive was intended primarily to improve traction and safety on the road; the fact that it gave credible off-road performance was very much a secondary consideration at the design stage. In support of this, the 4ETS four-wheel traction control system was part of the standard specification, using the ABS system (by now expected of every Mercedes) to restrain spinning wheels and to allow the driver to keep control of the vehicle more easily. The ABS system itself was a four-channel type, which incorporated a special programme for use on loose surfaces off-road when low ratio was engaged in the transfer gearbox.

Above all, however, the new Mercedes SUV was designed to be fully practical in everyday use. To that end, it was a comfortable five-seater, with a flexible three-seater rear-bench arrangement to improve that practicality. The middle rear seat could be folded down to make a table between the outer seats, and the passenger side seat could be folded forwards completely to give extra length on one side of the load bay. The whole rear bench could also be moved forwards by just over 3in to enlarge the load area behind. As an optional extra, a third row of forward-facing seats could be fitted in the load bay. These folded up to the sides of the vehicle when not in use, just as in many existing 4×4 models. In fact, this option was not ready by the time of the W163's launch but

This cutaway showing the 2001 model ML's interior makes clear that many of the 4×4 cues favoured by other SUV manufacturers had been abandoned in favour of a car-like atmosphere.

followed a few months afterwards. For early buyers who had missed out, a retro-fit could be arranged.

Partly as a way of keeping the showroom price down and partly because this was the traditional Mercedes way, cloth was chosen as the standard upholstery material. Leather was of course to be an option, coupled with electric adjustment and heating for the front seats. There would be walnut trim, a trip computer, a tiltable steering wheel, an auto-dimming mirror and a lockable safe box under the driver's seat, too.

The first the outside world got to see of the new Mercedes SUV was at the Detroit Motor Show, which opened on 3 January 1996. The vehicle was then still some months away from production, but, as Mercedes had announced nearly three years earlier that it would use its new US factory to build an SUV, the show car was hardly a surprise. It was typical of such Mercedes-Benz 'concepts' in the 1990s, however, that what went on display in Detroit was not exactly what the public was going to get later.

Mercedes billed it as an AAV ('All-Activity Vehicle'), partly to distance it from existing SUVs and partly to suggest that there was something very new about it. The show car did in fact provide a very good idea of what could be expected to come from the Tuscaloosa plant in a year or so's time, but its off-road toughness had been deliberately exaggerated with flared wheel arches, wide tyres and other features. Although specially built for the show, the AAV concept vehicle was in fact heavily based on the Californian design proposal that had been one of the five considered for production some two years earlier. And it was interesting that wide tyres were considered an essential part of the recipe for the USA: on the first production models, 255/65 tyres were fitted for the US market while 225/75s were considered adequate for Europe. The fatter tyres generated more road noise, and US models had extra sound insulation in the rear wheel wells to counteract this.

Mercedes had one further promotional trick up its sleeve to aid the introduction of the new vehicle, which by now had been given the marketing name of 'M class' – although all variants would in fact be badged as 'ML'

All the ambience of a luxury car: the dash of a 2004-model ML, one of the last before the new model was introduced.

SUV territory: Mercedes reasoned that most ML owners would not want to use their vehicles on terrain much more demanding than that shown in this picture. However, the ML's successor was made available with an optional 'off-road package', which suggests that some buyers wanted more than the first-generation model had to offer. The model pictured is the staple diesel of the range, an ML270 CDI.

because Stuttgart feared confusion with the strong M Series brand of high-performance cars from BMW. The company had secured for it a role in the forthcoming Steven Spielberg movie, *The Lost World: Jurassic Park*, which was the follow-up to the hugely successful first *Jurassic Park* movie. The basis of Michael Crichton's Jurassic Park stories is that a scientist has successfully re-created extinct dinosaurs from preserved DNA, and keeps them in a kind of dinosaur theme park – the Jurassic Park – on an island. This island is patrolled by game wardens, who need tough 4×4s for the job, and it was here that the Mercedes-Benz marketing people had spotted their opportunity.

Six very early production W163s were specially prepared for the job by the Mercedes-Benz Advanced Design Studios in Irvine, California, being given appropriate protective additions and painted in a sort of jungle green camouflage. There were three different styles, two of each type being built, and some of the film vehicles were used at motor

shows to help promote the launch of the M class. No production M class ever looked quite like these vehicles, but they were instantly recognizable for what they were. Their presence in the film undoubtedly did a great deal in enhancing public awareness of the new model and in giving it an image of toughness that its final appearance might otherwise not have suggested.

The new M class went on sale in 1998, US customers unsurprisingly getting examples a few months before sales began in Europe and elsewhere. For the USA, there was just one model at first, the 218bhp ML320 with a V6 petrol engine, although the range-topping ML430 with 268bhp 4.3-litre V8 followed not long afterwards. The V8 was worth the wait for those who wanted a high-performance machine. Its 7.9-second 0–60mph time knocked nearly two seconds off the 9.8 seconds posted by the ML320, although the extra 50bhp brought only a 3mph increase in maximum speed, from 194km/h (121mph) to 198km/h (124mph).

Central to the petrol-engined ML range was the 3.2-litre V6, which was of course used in a variety of other Mercedes models of the period. This is what the engine actually looked like…

… and this is what the engine looked like under the sloping bonnet of the ML. There was really very little to see apart from that characteristically neat plastic engine cover.

For Europe and other countries that began to take M class deliveries in the autumn, there were two more choices. First was an entry-level petrol model, the ML230, with the 150bhp four-cylinder M111 engine and a unique design of flat-faced five-spoke alloy wheels. Second was the ML270 CDI, with the 163bhp OM612 five-cylinder turbocharged diesel engine whose high torque output made the model a very respectable performer. Top speed was only 230km/h (114mph) and 0–60mph took 11.4 seconds, but these figures were well within expectations for full-sized diesel 4×4s in Europe and of course the ML270 CDI brought the advantage of far better fuel economy than its petrol brothers and, therefore, lower running costs.

The Mercedes designers and engineers had indeed got it right. The M class proved a substantial success both in the USA and elsewhere, although it was plagued at first with variable build quality. Some commentators suggested that this was the result of being built in the USA rather than Germany, but that was an uncharitable reflection on the abilities of the workforce in Alabama, who were, of course, reinforced by German colleagues on

attachment. The sad truth was that all Mercedes models were beginning to suffer from build quality problems at the time, and that the M class was no exception.

The basic design of the M class remained unchanged, and the W163 progressed on to the next logical stage, which was a high-performance derivative. In went the superb AMG-developed 5.5-litre V8 to make a 347bhp model called the ML55 AMG in 2000. With a maximum speed of 234km/h (146mph) and a 0–60mph time of 6.8 seconds, this would always remain the top performer of the M class range, and its high purchase and running costs of course helped to assure both its rarity and its exclusivity value.

What the ML55 AMG did, of course, was to confirm the demand for high-performance derivatives of the M class. One consequence was that the ML430 went out of production in 2001, to be replaced by the ML500. This boasted the 5-litre version of Mercedes' modular V8, its 292bhp delivering a maximum speed of 219km/h (137mph) while its ample torque promised acceleration from 0–60mph in just 7.7 seconds.

With the AMG model came some special

The ML55 AMG was initially shown as a concept, but everybody knew that it was destined for production unless there was a violent public reaction against it. This is the rather special dash of the show car.

features, most noticeably a more aggressively styled front apron and unique five-spoke alloy wheels on fatter tyres. Coinciding with its introduction, the rest of the 2002 model range underwent the usual Mercedes mid-life face-lift. There was another restyled front apron, this time incorporating driving lamps, and both front and rear bumper-and-apron assemblies went from matt grey plastic to body-colour paint.

It was the turn of the diesel range to be upgraded next, and from the early summer of 2002 there was a second diesel-powered model for some European countries (although not for the UK). This was the ML400 CDI, powered by the OM628 4-litre diesel engine and wearing new six-spoke alloy wheels. Its function was to deliver a high-performance diesel variant of the range, and in that it succeeded only too well. Acceleration to 60mph took just 8.7 seconds and there was strong torque right across the rev range, although fuel economy could suffer badly from enthusiastic use.

Quite clearly, the ML320 was next in line for a performance update, but it was not until 2003 that the model was replaced by the ML350, with the bigger 3.7-litre V6 engine and 235bhp. Maximum speed was 205km/h (128mph), and 60mph came up from rest in

This cutaway picture was produced to help promote the ML400 CDI model, but it shows the overall layout common to all variants.

ABOVE: The ML55 AMG looked pretty much like other models in the range, but it packed a massive V8 punch under its bonnet.

RIGHT: The ML500 replaced the ML430 in 2001, when it became clear that customers wanted high performance.

The ML was made available with the 4-litre V8 turbodiesel engine as an ML400 CDI – and the big engine put it into a different league from the ML270 CDI that was the only diesel available in most countries.

How Fast? How Thirsty?

These figures are typical for W163 ML models, but variations in the car's equipment levels and load, and variations in driving style will cause differences that may be significant.

	0–60mph	Max speed	Mpg (overall)
ML270 CDI (auto)	11.6secs	230km/h (114mph)	30 (9.4ltr/100km)
ML320	9.5secs	194km/h (121mph)	20 (14ltr/100km)
ML350	9.1secs	203km/h (127mph)	22 (12.8ltr/100km)
ML430	7.9secs	208km/h (130mph)	20 (14ltr/100km)
ML500	7.7secs	225km/h (140mph)	19 (31.4ltr/100km)
ML55 AMG	6.0secs	234km/h (146mph)	19 (31.4ltr/100km)

Best Buys

Various factors can influence purchase costs from time to time, and it is not possible to take these into account here. However, in terms of practicality and enjoyment, these are the best ML models to buy.

In European markets, diesel engines have always been strongly favoured for the ML. The high-performance ML400 CDI was unfortunately not made available in every market (the UK being one of those that did not get it) and so the only real choice has to fall on the ML270 CDI. Automatic transmission suits the vehicle best, although manuals were available.

If petrol power is the preferred choice (as, for example, in the USA), then the ML350 and ML430 are the best bets. They have very different characters, and there is a greater difference in their running costs than the relatively small difference in fuel consumption would suggest. The V8-powered ML430 is plenty quick enough for most people's needs and only the most determined buyer should hold out for the quicker and thirstier ML500. As for the ML55 AMG, this is a rare treat but really cannot be enjoyed to the full outside the derestricted Autobahns of Germany.

The wide air intake of the facelifted models made them look less gawky from the front and considerably more purposeful.

Blackout glass to the rear of the vehicle became fashionable during the ML's lifetime. Once the preserve of VIPs and drug dealers, it turned out to appeal to those who wanted to leave items on the back seat of the car and not have them stolen.

9.1 seconds, so the model was usefully quicker than its predecessor but did not disrupt the performance hierarchy of V6, V8 and AMG V8.

The ML270 CDI meanwhile plodded on, selling to large numbers of contented customers outside the USA and remaining the strongest-selling version of the M class in Europe. The six models – ML 230, ML270 CDI, ML350, ML400 CDI, ML500 and ML55 AMG – saw the range to a close in 2005, when

the W163 was replaced across the board by a second-generation M class model. It had sold in satisfyingly large volumes world-wide – a gratifying result for an all-new Mercedes model – and had established the Mercedes-Benz marque as a serious player in the SUV market. In the first decade of the twenty-first century, a variety of new models would capitalize on the advantage that the ML had created.

Specifications for W163 Models

Engines

Petrol models

ML230	2295cc M111 4-cyl, 150PS & 220Nm	(1998–2000)
ML320	3199cc M112 V6, 218PS & 310Nm	(1997–2005)
ML350	3724cc M112 V6, 235PS & 345Nm	(2002–2005)
ML430	4266cc M113 V8, 272PS & 390Nm	(1998–2001)
ML500	4966cc M113 V8, 292PS & 440Nm	(2001–2005)
ML55 AMG	5439cc M113 V8, 347PS & 510Nm	(1999–2005)

Diesel models

ML270 CDI	2685cc OM612 5-cyl, 163PS & 370Nm	(1999–2005)
	Automatic models with 400Nm	
ML400 CDI	3996cc OM628 V8, 250PS & 560Nm	(2001–2005)

Transmissions
Five-speed manual (ML230 only)
Six-speed manual
Five-speed automatic

Running gear
Front suspension with double wishbones, torsion bars, twin-tube gas dampers and anti-roll bar.
Rear suspension with double wishbones, coil springs, twin-tube gas dampers and anti-roll bar.
Power-assisted rack-and-pinion steering.
Power-assisted brakes with ABS as standard; ventilated discs at the front and solid discs at the rear.

Dimensions
Overall length: 4587mm (180.5in) (to 2001, except ML55 AMG); 4635mm (182.5in) (ML55 AMG from 2001); 4638mm (182.5in) pre-2001 ML55 AMG and all other post-2001 models

Wheelbase: 2820mm (111in)
Overall width: 1840mm (72in)
Overall height: 1804–1820mm (71–71.5in), depending on tyre choice
Track: 1555mm (61in) front and rear

Weights (typical)
ML230:	1930kg (4246lb)
ML320:	2010kg (4422lb)
ML430:	2100kg (4620lb)
ML270 CDI to 2001:	2115kg (4653lb)
ML270 CDI from 2001:	2175kg (4785lb)
ML350:	2185kg (4807lb)
ML500:	2210kg (4862lb)
ML55AMG:	2230kg (4906lb)
ML400 CDI:	2335kg (5137lb)

11 S Class Splendour

The W220 Saloons

By the time work began on the successor to the W140 S class models in 1993, it was already clear that something radically different would be required. The W140 had failed to catch the mood of the times (*see* Chapter 4), and – worse in some ways – it was to some eyes an unattractive and ostentatious lump of a car. Rivals from BMW, Audi, and Lexus exploited this weakness in the Mercedes-Benz line-up, and made inroads into traditional Mercedes territory that the Stuttgart manufacturer would take several years to claw back.

As a result, there were two groups of factors that influenced the design of the next-generation S class, which Stuttgart knew as the W220. The first group reflected Mercedes' own aims of improving on its own products;

these were factors such as the search for more power, more safety, and more space. The second group reflected that need to put right the mistakes of the W140; these were factors such as the search for better economy, better looks, and less weight. Some of the factors in the second group tended to work against those in the first. It was a tall order.

Despite the obvious challenges, the new W220, introduced at the Paris Motor Show in 1998, succeeded brilliantly. It not only won back leadership of the top luxury saloon market for Mercedes, but it also earned praise all over the world for its curvaceous good looks. Even at the time of writing, some years after the end of production, the W220 remains a good-looking car; indeed, many observers would argue that it is better-looking than its W221 successor.

The W220 was quite possibly one of Mercedes' best-looking saloons ever, and its well-balanced lines contrasted sharply with those of the bulky-looking W140 that it replaced.

173

Size Mattered

The W220 was drawn up around an interior package which provided an extra 37mm (1.5in) of cabin length as compared with the W140. Yet the car's overall dimensions were smaller in every way: the wheelbase of 2965mm (117in) was 75mm (3in) shorter than the W140's; the overall length of 5043mm (198in) saved 60mm (just over 2in); 29mm (just over an inch) had been shaved off the width, and the car stood 44mm lower (1.75in).

The lines of the body made the car look even smaller. Curvaceous, even sensuous, they made it look almost sporty. Careful attention to aerodynamics had delivered a Cd that averaged 0.27 across the range, a figure which set a new standard for cars in this class.

This reduction in size had certainly contributed to a quite dramatic reduction in weight, which averaged out at 300kg (660lb) across the range, or around 15 per cent. However, an equally important factor was the strategic use of alloys, composites and high-strength steels in the car's construction. These same choices of construction material were also important in improving the crash-resistance of the body shell.

This all-new shell – planned from the start to have standard, long, and ultra-long wheel-base derivatives – rode on a suspension system that was new to Mercedes. Known as Airmatic, this electronically controlled air suspension gave a superb ride in all conditions. It was very different indeed from the air suspension that Mercedes had used in the 1960s and had then abandoned as too costly and too troublesome.

There were conventional steel coil springs to support the car's static weight, but when in motion the body shell was supported on rubber bellows at each wheel. The air pressure in these could be varied automatically to provide self-levelling, and (like the less sophisticated system introduced in the Range Rover during 1992) to lower the ride height by 15mm (just over half an inch) at speed for greater stability. There was also a manual over-ride system, allowing the car to be raised by 35mm (just over an inch and a quarter) on its air springs to negotiate obstacles such as road humps or parking ramps. Manual control also permitted a choice of 'sport' and 'comfort' settings, and

The W220 was a good-looking car from any angle, and its handling was an unexpected delight for a car of its size. Note the indicator repeaters on the door mirrors – a feature that was pioneered on these cars and swiftly copied by manufacturers all over the world.

The S class has traditionally included a long-wheelbase saloon model, which enjoyed the same harmonious styling as the standard-wheelbase cars. The extra length was all in the rear doors.

the system was combined with ADS (Adaptive Damper Control) to even out the ride over all but the most severe surfaces.

Most of the braking and traction control systems fitted as standard were only to be expected in an S class Mercedes by this stage. They included ABS, ASR, BAS and ESP. The brake discs were now made of a composite of steel and aluminium. However, new to the party was power-assisted rack-and-pinion steering. This had been adopted partly because it gave better steering 'feel' and contributed to more sporty handling, but also because the packaging of the rack allowed better front-end

The entry-level petrol engine for the W220 range was the 2.8-litre in the S280.

The W220's sleek shape was arguably one of the best ever to come from Mercedes, and made the car look smaller than it really was. This is an S500.

crash performance. With the older recirculating-ball system that Mercedes had favoured for so long, it would have been necessary to add several millimetres of length to the front of the car in order to get the necessary protection.

Equipment levels were very high. In addition to the expected two front airbags, there were airbags in the doors and in the cantrail at the sides of the car, in each case to reduce the risk of injury to the occupants in a side impact. Distronic intelligent cruise control (which automatically kept the car a set distance from the one in front) was standard, along with the Keyless Go system, which, as it name suggests, did away with the need for keys to unlock and start the car.

A new automatic climate-control system – the first of its kind in a car – maintained a set temperature in the cabin by means of sensors; it was even 'intelligent' enough to take account of sun on one side of the car and to provide extra cooling on that side. There were even Active Ventilated Seats, which provided cool air through perforations in their covers when

needed, in addition, of course, to providing warmth through electric heating pads. Double-glazing and electric door closing, both standard on the W140s, were however relegated to extra-cost items.

One very significant advance was the new COMAND system. The initials stood for Cockpit Management and Data, and the interface with the car's occupants was a video screen on the central instrument stack. COMAND provided controls for all the car's ventilation, navigation, audio and communication systems from a series of buttons around the edge of the screen. Some of these systems, of course, were optional extras, as was the new Linguatronic voice recognition and command system, which obviated the need for pressing any buttons at all.

Many first buyers of a W220 S class Mercedes were probably not too concerned about what was under the bonnet, as long as the figures on the boot lid were sufficiently prestigious. However, the initial release of W220s at the Paris Show consisted of three petrol models – the S320, S430, and S500. All of these models could be had in both standard- and long-wheelbase forms, the latter with an extra 120mm (4.75in) of legroom for the rear-seat passengers. A couple of months later, in December, they were joined by an S280 that was available only with the standard wheelbase and for certain export markets. These included the UK.

All these engines were the new three-valve types that had made their bow in the W210 E class and the R129 SLs. Those in the S280 and S320 were M112 V6s, offering 204PS and 224 PS respectively. The S430 and S500 models were powered by M113 V8s, the smaller engine delivering 279PS and the larger one 306PS. Optional for the V8s was Active Cylinder Control, which deactivated four cylinders at cruising speeds to save fuel. The V8s provided more than ample power and torque, but the V6s – especially the 2.8-litre – had to work quite hard to earn their keep. In every case, the only gearbox option was a five-speed automatic with Tip-shift manual over-ride. The W5A 330 (with a maximum torque tolerance of 330Nm)

was fitted behind the two V6 engines, but the stronger W5A 580 (with a 580Nm tolerance) was used with the V8s.

1999–2001: Expanding the Options

With the basic range established and well received, Mercedes now turned to the models they probably perceived as 'fringe' types. They could have been forgiven for imagining that the diesel derivative would not be a strong seller, as the diesel W140s had sold in relatively small quantities, and that is probably why they waited until November 1999 before making available the S320 CDI. In fact, the excellence of the new common-rail diesel engine in this model rapidly earned it a strong following, especially in European countries, including the UK, where it became the best-seller of the W220 range.

Before the S320 CDI made its appearance, however, an AMG derivative was announced. From March 1999, those with the wherewithal and the need for speed could buy the S55 AMG, which was powered by the long-stroke

The AMG models of course had their own interior ambience, with dark grey wood trim. This is the cabin of a long-wheelbase S55 Kompressor.

AMG development of the M113 5-litre V8 that had already been announced for the W210 E class. It delivered 360PS and huge torque of 530Nm and would rocket to 60mph in 6 seconds. AMG had worked on the engine's breathing, fitted hotter camshafts, increased the size of the brake discs, and added fatter tyres on 18in wheels. Officially limited to 250km/h (155mph), the car was nevertheless capable of some 282km/h (176mph) if the speed limiter was removed – which AMG were only too happy to do. Such performance in a big luxury saloon – a long-wheelbase S55 AMG was available as well as the standard-wheelbase car – might appear to be something that would interest very few people, but there was never a lack of customers. In the two years of its availability, no fewer than 2300 examples of the car were sold, which was an excellent result for an AMG product.

The new diesel engine nevertheless had far more impact on the W220 range as a whole. Just as the new AMG engine had first appeared in the W210 E class, so the OM613 six-cylinder diesel had made its debut in the E320 CDI a few months before it was announced for the

S class. It was light years ahead of the oil-burners that had powered the old W140 S class, a quiet, refined engine with a huge 470Nm of torque that gave the W220 almost sporting acceleration. The car could reach 60mph from rest in 8.8 seconds – quick for any size of car at that stage – and peaked at 230km/h (143mph), which was quite fast enough for most users. Fuel economy was also good for a luxury saloon, and the bills were all the more palatable in those countries where diesel was subject to lower taxation than petrol.

The flagship of the range was yet to come. There had been a V12-powered S600 in the W140 range, and Mercedes had every intention of following this with a V12 edition of the W220. Indeed, they had said as much at the time of the model's launch, suggesting that it would reach the market in 2000. And so it did. The S600 was announced in long-wheelbase form only during January 2000.

The V12 engine that powered it was not the complex M120 engine that had entered production in 1991. That was old technology as far as Stuttgart was concerned. The W220 S600 came with a brand-new V12 known as the

Discreet, luxurious, but above all supremely functional, this is the fascia of a 2001-model W220.

LEFT: The V12-powered S600 came as standard with the long-wheelbase body shell... and with the distinctive alloy wheels seen in this picture. Otherwise, it was as discreet as top-model Mercedes always have been.

RIGHT: Another feast for the eyes – though perhaps not quite a garage mechanic's delight! This is the flagship V12 engine in a 2001 S600 model.

BELOW: The side marker light at the corner of the front bumper identifies this S600 as one for the US market.

Very exclusive indeed was the Pullman limousine on an extended wheelbase, seen here as an S500 model. It was not a six-door car – that would have carried the taint of a common airport taxi – but that centre section had fixed panels.

M137. The cylinders were once again arranged in a 60-degree vee and the block was again made of aluminium, but almost everything else had changed. The swept volume was in fact nearer 5.8 litres than the 6 litres that the car's name suggested, the bore being smaller and the stroke longer than their equivalents in the older engine. Instead of two camshafts on each cylinder bank and four valves for each cylinder, there was a single camshaft for each bank and a three-valve layout like that used on the M112 V6s and M113 V8s. It saved weight, cost and complication.

Despite variable timing on both camshafts (it was only on the inlet camshafts of the earlier V12), the new lightweight engine was less powerful than the one it replaced. The power of 367PS looked poor against the 408PS of the old M120, and the torque of 530Nm was way down on the 580Nm found in the old S600. But the new car's lower weight and better aerodynamics helped, and no customer would have had cause for complaint. The W220 S600 accelerated to 60mph from standstill in 6.3 seconds as compared to 6.6 seconds for the older car. Both were, of course, restricted to 250km/h (155mph), and the overall fuel consumption of the newer model was very noticeably better.

With the arrival of the new flagship model, Stuttgart was able to expand the range still further. During 2000, it introduced both Pullman and armoured long-wheelbase variants of the S600 and the S500. Both were, of course, built in very limited numbers. The armoured models, known as Guard types, were available with two levels of ballistic protection, to B4 or B6/B7 standard. It was part of their *raison d'être* that they should look like standard long-wheelbase models, and indeed they did.

The Pullman was a different matter. Pullman models sat on a wheelbase that had been extended to 4085mm (161in) – a full metre longer than that of the long-wheelbase models. All of that extra space went into the rear compartment, and the gap between the front and rear doors was made up by a fixed body side panel. There were probably as many different variations on the layout of the extra cabin space as there were customers for the car, but in every case the cars were trimmed to match the already opulent S class cabin trim so that the car did not appear to be anything as vulgar as a mere 'stretch limo'. The price was a secret that Stuttgart never disclosed – it probably depended very much on the customer's choice of specification.

Stuttgart was not finished with new models yet. Stung into action by the introduction of turbocharged V8 diesels from Audi and BMW, its engineers had been working on just such an engine to provide the S class with a diesel flagship. A prototype engine had been shown as a 'concept' at the 1997 Frankfurt Show in a W210 E class (*see* Chapter 6), but the W220 was the first production application for the new OM628.

Unusually for a V8, this new engine had its

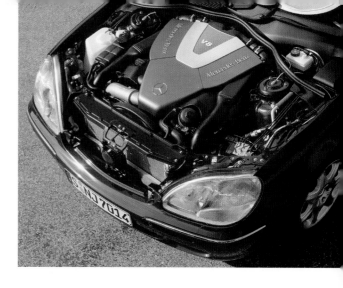

cylinder banks in a 75-degree vee. The block was made of weight-saving aluminium, and there was common-rail direct injection and one overhead camshaft per cylinder bank but four valves for each cylinder. There were twin turbochargers and an intercooler. With 250PS at a low 4000rpm and a massive 560Nm of torque all the way from 1800rpm to 2600rpm, this was another astounding technological leap forward by Mercedes. The S400 CDI that carried it needed just 7.8 seconds to reach 60mph and would forge on to a 250km/h (155mph) top speed. Arguably, this new diesel model made the smaller petrol-engined cars redundant, but certain important markets such as the USA were firmly wedded to V8 petrol engines. The S400 CDI was not made available in every Mercedes market and seems to have been something of an acquired taste. Build volumes stuck at around 1300 a year.

The S400 CDI was the last new W220 introduction from Stuttgart before the range received its mid-life makeover in 2002. Down in Affalterbach, however, AMG had been busily preparing a model to replace the S55 AMG,

As usual, there was little to see when the V8 diesel was installed in the car, except for a neat and tidy-looking engine bay. This is a 2001 model.

and in November 2001 they announced it with the name of S63 AMG.

As its name suggested, this car had a 6.3-litre engine. Rather than continuing to develop the M113 V8 (which AMG found difficult to tune), the company had turned to the new M137 V12. Both bore and stroke were increased, to give a swept volume of 6258cc;

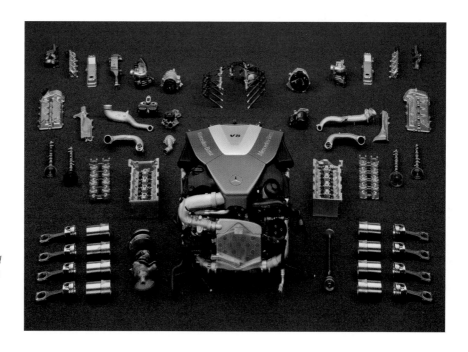

Mercedes were very proud of the 4-litre V8 diesel in the S400 CDI – and rightly so. This is the engine with some of its key components.

The V8 turbodiesel model was never available in right-hand-drive markets, but sold well in those countries where diesel fuel remained cheaper than petrol. From the outside, only the badges on the boot lid gave it away – those and the growl of that powerful diesel engine.

This cutaway shows the layout of the 4-litre diesel V8 with its common-rail direct injection fuel system.

power went up to 444PS and torque to 620Nm. AMG would have liked more, but the three-valve configuration created the same gas-flow problems as it had in the V8s. So customers had to settle for a 5.7-second 0–60mph time and a 250km/h (155mph) top speed – unless, of course, they asked AMG to remove the speed restrictor. Supposedly, 278km/h (174mph) was then possible – the sort of speed that may be worth bragging about at the golf club but is simply not realistically achievable on ordinary roads in most countries. All the S63 models were sold in Europe and Asia, and the car's production run of around a year ensured it would always be rare.

The 2002 Mid-Life Makeover

The W220 needed very little in the way of cosmetic changes when it was due for its mid-life makeover. Although Stuttgart did make a

number of modifications to the cars in autumn 2002, they were very subtle ones.

The front end took on a new grille, which was broader, taller and more upright than the old one – although it was difficult to tell the difference unless the two were set side by side. There were larger air intakes in the front apron, and the bumper inserts were lengthened so that they finished closer to the number-plate. Their Parktronic sensors, all too visible on the earlier models, were also made more discreet. Meanwhile, the headlamps were changed to H7 types on the six-cylinder and V8 models, while the 600 went over to the very latest Bi-Xenon lamps.

At the rear, redesigned tail-light clusters offered a quicker way of identifying one of the new models. They now had four clear horizontal lens sections instead of the earlier two, and the red reflector at the bottom was more readily visible. Larger turn indicator lenses on

The first cars had tail lights with just two horizontal 'white' sections, as shown on this standard-wheelbase S320 CDI.

the door mirrors helped recognition from the side, while there were the inevitable new alloy wheel designs. On most models, these had a brighter finish than before; on the 600, the old five-hole design remained available as an option in place of the new six-hole design. Models with 16in wheels now had a steel disc-type spare, but those with 17in and 18in wheels had only a lightweight space-saver spare.

There were changes inside, too, most noticeably some extra chrome highlights. The front-seat bolsters now gave better comfort, and the COMAND systems control screen was enlarged and could optionally be combined with the APS satellite navigation system. Orthopaedic seats, a heated steering wheel, and an extra cupholder for the front-seat passenger were all new options.

What the customers could not see was the new suite of safety measures known as Pre-Safe. These depended, like so many items on the Mercedes models of this period, on

A sunroof was not a standard feature, as this long-wheelbase S320 makes clear.

electronics. In essence, sensors around the car detected an impending crash (from such indications as sudden fierce braking or a sudden change in the car's attitude) and triggered a number of automatic reactions. Seat belts were tightened, the passenger seats returned to their upright positions to give maximum occupant protection, and the sunroof closed. If there was no crash and the situation returned to normal, Pre-Safe automatically returned everything to its earlier position.

There was a further invisible safety aid available if customers were prepared to pay for it: the 4MATIC four-wheel-drive system, which had not previously been available on S class models. Its introduction in 2002 had been prompted largely by the success of Quattro (four-wheel-drive) versions of the Audi A8, which had been a big hit in the USA.

The 4MATIC system was already available on less expensive models in the Mercedes range, and notably on the W210 E class. These cars had been developed mainly for sale in the Alpine regions of Europe, where their extra sure-footedness was especially welcome dur-

The outboard 'projector' light behind the elegantly curved glass was new for the 2002 model-year.

ing the snowy season. It was a relatively simple task to adapt the technology to suit the W220, and from spring 2002 both standard-wheelbase and long-wheelbase versions of the S350 4MATIC, S430 4MATIC and S500 4MATIC were made available. Why was there no equivalent with the V12 engine? Presumably, Mercedes had decided that likely sales would

Later models incorporated some changes to the layout of the controls, most noticeable on the centre console of this 2004 example.

The key components of the 4MATIC four-wheel-drive system as used on an S350 model are seen here. The extra propshaft ran to the front differential from a set of transfer gears on the back of the main gearbox.

This is the layout of the front-wheel drivetrain of a 4MATIC system as used in the W220 S class. In this case, the engine is the 4.3-litre V8 of an S430 model.

not justify the cost of developing such a car, which would certainly have been an expensive and complex beast. Strangely, there were no diesel 4MATIC models, either.

For many observers, though, the most important changes at that 2002 watershed were under the bonnet. Out went the old 3.2-litre M112 V6 engine, to be replaced by a big-bore 3.7-litre, although the car it powered was

somewhat illogically given the S350 designation. Changes to the 3.2-litre diesel brought more power and torque, together with the new OM648 designation. However, the major changes were at the top of the W220 range.

On the performance side, the AMG model

The four all-white horizontal segments of the 2002 and later tail lights are clearly visible on this S500 4MATIC.

now came with the Affalterbach company's supercharged 5.5-litre V8 engine as an S55 Kompressor AMG. This engine had been introduced in autumn 2001 for the latest SL range (the R230 models, not covered in this book) and was a breathtakingly powerful derivative of the older 5.5-litre naturally aspirated type. The key to its extra performance was a Japanese-made Lysholm-type supercharger mounted in the vee between the cylinder banks – AMG's solution to the difficulties of tuning the three-valve M113 engine – but of course a number of key components in the engine had also been beefed up to take the extra strain. The massive 700Nm torque output had also demanded work on the gearbox, and although this started life as a W5A 580 type it had actually been considerably strengthened. Even the long-wheelbase derivative of the car could hit 60mph from rest in an outrageous 4.8 seconds, but the AMG car remained discreet from the outside. Only alloy wheels with five twin spokes, four tailpipes peeping out beneath the rear bumper, and badging on front wings and boot lid gave

onlookers any idea that this was no ordinary S class saloon.

However, Mercedes had no intention of letting its in-house tuner steal all the limelight. New for the 600 model was a brand-new V12 engine – Mercedes' third generation of the type – which boasted twin turbochargers. This engine (of which a derivative was also planned for the Maybach super-saloon) delivered performance that lifted the Mercedes way beyond its obvious rivals from BMW and Audi, promising the same 4.8-second 0–60mph acceleration as the supercharged AMG car but with a silken rather than sporting feel. Like the supercharged AMG car, the new 600 had an uprated transmission, in this case the W5A 900 type that had been developed to handle the planned 900Nm of the Maybach V12 engine.

2003: The Final Upgrades

Stuttgart was not quite done with the W220 range, although its W221 successor was already in the final stages of its development. One item

---

How Fast? How Thirsty?

These figures are typical for W220 S class models, but variations in the car's equipment levels and load, and variations in driving style will cause differences that may be significant.

	0–60mph	Max speed	Mpg (overall)
S280	9.7sec	230km/h (143mph)	24 (11.8ltr/100km)
S320	8.2sec	238km/h (149mph)	22 (12.8ltr/100km)
S320 CDI	8.8sec	230km/h (143mph)	28 (10ltr/100km)
S350	7.6sec	245km/h (153mph)	23 (12.3ltr/100km)
S400 CDI	7.8sec	250km/h (155mph)	26 (10.8ltr/100km)
S430	7.3sec	250km/h (155mph) (limited)	21 (13.5ltr/100km)
S500	6.5sec	250km/h (155mph) (limited)	19 (31.4ltr/100km)
S600	6.3sec	250km/h (155mph) (limited)	18 (15.7ltr/100km)
S55 AMG	6.0sec	250km/h (155mph) (limited)	
		280km/h (174mph) (unlimited)	18 (15.7ltr/100km)
S55 AMG Kompressor	4.8sec	250km/h (155mph) (limited)	
		280km/h (174mph) (unlimited)	19 (31.4ltr/100km)
S65 AMG	4.5sec	250km/h (155mph) (limited)	
		298km/h (186mph) (unlimited)	16 (17.5ltr/100km)

intended for the new car was a seven-speed automatic gearbox, and from spring 2003 this was introduced – tried out, perhaps – in the V8 models of the W220 range. Known to the engineers as the W7A 700, but marketed as the 7G-Tronic, this offered extremely smooth shifts and even delivered marginally better fuel economy than the old five-speed type. Gears one to five were lower than before, to offset the effect of a taller axle ratio (which now shared the 2.65:1 ratio of the latest S600), but sixth and seventh were tall ratios and allowed lower engine revs at high speeds and, therefore, lower fuel consumption.

The final word on the W220s, though, went to AMG. It was more or less inevitable that Mercedes' performance division would get to work on the latest V12 engine, and at the Chicago Motor Show in February 2003 they showed the fruits of their labours. Unashamedly aimed at the US market, it was called the S65 AMG, although the '65' was indicative only of the fact that it delivered

---

Best Buys

Various factors can influence purchase costs from time to time, and it is not possible to take these into account here. However, in terms of practicality and enjoyment, these are the best W220 S class models to buy.

The AMG models and the V12 S600 are assured of long-term desirability on the grounds that they were the top models of the W220 range and also the rarest. However, for real-world buyers an S500 will offer more than enough – unless fuel economy is an important factor.

It was fuel economy that made the S320 CDI diesels such a popular choice when they were new, and their more than adequate performance and high levels of refinement will ensure that they remain a good buy even when other W220 models have descended to 'banger' status. Of the petrol models, the S350 is perhaps the best of the bunch, eclipsing even the otherwise excellent S320 in its acceleration and fuel economy.

---

more than the S63 AMG it replaced. In fact, the engine's capacity remained unchanged from the factory-standard 5980cc, but changes to the turbochargers and the management system (among other things) had enabled it to produce an astounding 1000Nm of torque all the way from 2000rpm to 4000rpm, with a maximum power of 612PS.

Foot-to-the-floor, the S65 knocked 0.3 seconds off the 0–60mph acceleration of a standard S600. Those 0.3 seconds cost the car's purchaser some 70,000 Euros on top of the cost of a standard S600; this car was clearly intended for those who had enough money to have the best – full stop. Not many were built, and most probably went to the USA, although at least one right-hand-drive car found a buyer in Britain and could occasionally be seen flogging through the London traffic during the rush-hour.

The S65 was nevertheless a discreet creation, easy enough for the man in the street to mistake for any other W220. Enthusiasts would spot its boot-lid badging and four chrome-tipped tailpipes, of course, and perhaps the small 'V12 Biturbo' badges on the front wings, and the special five-spoke 19in alloy wheels with 245/40 tyres on the front wheels and 275/35 tyres on the rears. An AMG front apron with broad meshed air intake and AMG side skirts were further giveaways. A closer look would show the huge two-piece brake discs, each 15.2in in diameter, with their eight-piston fixed calipers, and a peep inside might also reveal the 360km/h (225mph) speedometer – although the car was electronically limited to the usual 250km/h (155mph).

The final W220s were built over the summer of 2005. Their successors, the W221 series, had already been announced with the usual array of improvements, and quickly proved a hit with buyers. They were definitely not as attractive as the W220s, however, and it is arguable that the 1998–2005 S class will go down in history as one of Stuttgart's best-looking creations ever.

AMG's 5.5-litre V8 in the S class saloon body produced the extraordinarily rapid S55 AMG. It was discreet, too, although special sills, front apron and those paired exhaust outlets gave the game away to those who knew what to look for. The 'V8 Kompressor' badge on each front wing was a further clue.

Specifications for W220 Models

Engines

Petrol models

S280	2799cc M112 V6-cyl, 204PS & 270Nm	(1999–2005)
S280 (LWB)	2799cc M112 V6-cyl, 204PS & 270Nm	(2002–2005)
S320	3199cc M112 V6-cyl, 224PS & 315Nm	(1998–2002)
S320 (LWB)	3199cc M112 V6-cyl, 224PS & 315Nm	(1998–2002)
S350	3724cc M112 V6-cyl, 245PS & 350Nm	(2002–2005)
S350 (LWB)	3724cc M112 V6-cyl, 245PS & 350Nm	(2002–2005)
S430	4266cc M113 V8-cyl, 279PS & 400Nm	(1998–2005)
S430 (LWB)	4266cc M113 V8-cyl, 279PS & 400Nm	(1998–2005)
S500	4966cc M113 V8-cyl, 306PS & 460Nm	(1998–2005)
S500 (LWB)	4966cc M113 V8-cyl, 306PS & 460Nm	(1998–2005)
S600	5786cc M137 V12-cyl, 367PS & 530Nm	(2000–2002)
	5513cc M275 V12-cyl, 500PS & 800Nm	(2002–2005)
S55 AMG	5439cc M113 V8-cyl, 360PS & 530Nm	(1999–2002)
S55 AMG (LWB)	5439cc M113 V8-cyl, 360PS & 530Nm	(1999–2002)
S55 AMG Kompressor	5439cc M113 V8-cyl, 500PS & 700Nm	(2002–2005)
S55 AMG Kompressor (LWB)	5439cc M113 V8-cyl, 500PS & 700Nm	(2002–2005)
S63 AMG	6258cc M137 V12-cyl, 444PS & 620Nm	(2001–2002)
S65 AMG	5980cc M275 V12-cyl, 600PS & 1000Nm	(2002–2005)

Diesel models

S320 CDI	3222cc OM613 6-cyl, 197PS & 470Nm	(1999–2002)
	3222cc OM648 6-cyl, 204PS & 500Nm	(2002–2005)
S320 CDI (LWB)	3222cc OM613 6-cyl, 197PS & 470Nm	(2002)
	3222cc OM648 6-cyl, 204PS & 500Nm	(2002–2005)
S400 CDI	3996cc OM628 V8, 250PS & 560Nm	(2000–2005)
S400 CDI (LWB)	3996cc OM628 V8, 250PS & 560Nm	(2002–2005)

Transmissions

Five-speed automatic
Seven-speed automatic from spring 2003 (S430 and S500 only)

Running gear

Front suspension with four links, height-adjustable air springs, air-operated dampers and anti-roll bar.
Multi-link rear suspension with height-adjustable air springs, air-operated dampers and anti-roll bar.
Power-assisted rack-and-pinion steering.
Power-assisted brakes with five-channel ABS as standard; ventilated discs at the front and solid discs at the rear.

Dimensions

Overall length: 5038mm (198in); 5158mm (203in) for long-wheelbase models

Wheelbase: 2965mm (117in); 3085mm (121in) for long-wheelbase models
Overall width: 1855mm (73in)
Overall height: 1444mm (57in)
Track: 1574mm (62in)

Weights (typical)

S280:	2300kg (5060lb)
S280 LWB:	2330kg (5126lb)
S320:	2300kg (5060lb)
S320 CDI:	2430kg (5346lb)
S350:	2340kg (5148lb)
S400 CDI:	2455kg (5401lb)
S430:	2380kg (5236lb)
S430 4Matic:	2505kg (5511lb)
S500:	2380kg (5236lb)
S600:	2590kg (5698lb)
S55 AMG:	2380kg (5236lb)

Index